KU-484-194

CONTENTS

INTRODUCTION

COUNSELLING

Before we launch into COGNITIVE behavioural ways of working, it might be helpful to take a look at some definitions of counselling itself. It is important to locate the helping activity of counselling in relation to other helping activities in order to avoid confusion regarding the purpose of this book. This book is specifically aimed at people wanting to learn about a COGNITIVE Behaviour Therapy (CBT) approach to counselling with no previous experience or knowledge of counselling or psychology. The key word here is counselling.

So what do we mean by counselling?

What is counselling for?

One way of defining counselling is to look at what it is useful for. In the past thirty years, counselling has become ubiquitous, and it is perilously close to being presented as a panacea for just about everything. Some critics say that the emerging 'profession' of counselling has much to gain for claiming, on behalf of counsellors and therapists, that counselling is good for everything. It would be wrong to make such claims: counselling has its limits and part of being a counsellor is to know what those limits are. The problem is that when we are in distress, it is comforting to think that there is a simple answer around the corner.

The situation is not made any easier when we understand that simply sitting down and taking time out from a busy life can make things seem better. Counsellors must be able to explain to their clients the differences between this very important relief and comfort that can be gained from compassionate human contact on the one hand, and counselling as a specialist activity on the other. Counselling can help people in certain states of distress and usually involves change:

- change in the way the client sees things or themselves
- change in the way a client thinks about things or themselves
- change in the way a client feels about things or themselves
- change in the way a client behaves

Although many people will not be able to put it neatly into a few words, what they seek from counselling can be roughly summarised in a few categories:

- support
- problem-solving
- developing new strategies
  for living
- recovery
- gaining insight or self-awareness

The sort of distress that counselling can help is often called 'emotional' or 'psychological' and can include:

- stress—a very general and possibly over-used term, but there are some situations in life, especially those that you can't control, that might leave you feeling so stressed that it interferes with your everyday life
- conflict—at home or work
- bereavement—whether a relative or friend. Indeed, having anything permanently taken away might lead to a feeling of bereavement, such as losing your job or losing your ability to do something like walk, play sport or have sex
- depression—another over-used term and not one to be taken lightly. Many life events can make us feel low, and talking it over really does help. The popular term 'depression' can cover everything from feeling understandably low after having your purse stolen or losing your job, through to being unable to get up in the morning or eat properly because you think life is not worth living
- coping with poor health, e.g. having a long-standing health problem or receiving a diagnosis of a serious or terminal illness
- trauma, e.g. surviving (including witnessing) something very disturbing (including abuse of various forms)

What counselling is not for

When someone decides to attend counselling sessions, they are, by definition, distressed. It is, therefore, particularly important that the client doesn't have either their time wasted or their distress increased by attending something that we might reasonably predict would be of no help.

As we have already seen, it is difficult to honestly predict whether counselling will definitely help in a particular circumstance. Nevertheless there are times when counselling is clearly not the first or only appropriate intervention. It is doubly difficult to appear to turn someone away when they arrive because sometimes:

- part of their distress might be that they have difficulty feeling understood and valued
- they may lack self-confidence and a rejection would damage it even more
- they have been to other types of helper and they think that counselling is their last hope
- they are so desperate they might consider suicide

However difficult it might be, we have to be completely honest with clients if we think counselling is not going to help. It would be wrong to let them find out after a number of sessions, after which they might feel that they are to blame for not trying hard enough. The use of counselling should be questioned if it is likely that their symptoms of distress are caused by:

- poor housing or homelessness
- lack of opportunity due to discrimination or oppression
- poverty

Problems of this nature are best addressed by social action. The counsellor as a citizen shares responsibility with all other members of society to remove these blocks to people's physical and psychological well-being.

It would be convenient if we could divide problems up into two neat categories; those of psychological origin (and amenable to counselling) and those of non-psychological origin (and therefore not amenable to counselling). However, there are some other causes of distress which, although they will not be *solved* by counselling, will undoubtedly be helped by counselling in that the person concerned will be able to function better with the kind of support that counselling can provide. It may also be that the client experiences repetitive patterns of self-defeating thoughts and behaviour which renders them less effective in dealing with problems which do not have a psychological origin. It might also be that a person would be better able to challenge an oppressive system if they felt personally empowered, and counselling can sometimes achieve this. Such problems include those caused by:

- poor health (a physical illness or organic condition)
- oppression and discrimination, including bullying
- living in an abusive relationship

Counsellors must be constantly vigilant to ensure that their work with a particular client or clients in general is not contributing to disadvantage, abuse and oppression by rendering people more acceptant of poor conditions, whether at work or at home.

> Psychologists must join with persons who reject racism, sexism, colonialism and exploitation and must find ways to redistribute social power and to increase social justice. PRIMARY PREVENTION RESEARCH inevitably will make clear the relationship between social pathology and PSYCHOPATHOLOGY and then will work to change social and political structures in the interests of social justice. It is as simple and as difficult as that! (Albee, 1996: 1131, cited in Davies & Burdett, 2004: 279)

What is 'personal growth'?

Counselling in the UK has become associated with what might be called the 'personal growth industry'. Self-improvement has been a feature of our society for a hundred years or more and includes such initiatives as the Workers' Education Association supporting the educational needs of working men and women. More recently further education has embraced more non-vocational courses and reflects the fact that as we get more affluent we have to attend less to the business of mere survival. We can turn our attention to getting more out of life and along with other self-development activities, improving our psychological well-being proves to be a popular choice. Furthermore, when people have a good experience as a client, they sometimes see that learning to be a counsellor could be a further step in self-improvement.

This 'personal growth' use of counselling contrasts with counselling as a treatment for more acute forms of psychological distress as listed on page 2 above. It is, however, no less worthy or ultimately useful. Fulfilled, happy citizens, relating positively to themselves and others, able to put good helping skills back into their communities are an asset, not a handicap.

WHAT IS COGNITIVE BEHAVIOUR THERAPY (CBT)?

COGNITIVE Behaviour Therapy (CBT) is one of many different types of 'talking therapies'. CBT is an *active-directive, collaborative* approach to dealing with emotional and psychiatric disorders. This means that CBT therapists talk directly to their clients and ask them direct questions. It also means that the client and therapist work together in a very overt manner to help the former overcome their presenting difficulties. In contrast to psychodynamic, PSYCHOANALYTICAL or person-centred schools of therapy, CBT is present focused, time bound, highly structured and goal orientated. This is *not* to imply that the other therapeutic modalities mentioned are not interested in structure and goals, but that CBT addresses these in a very obvious fashion. In CBT treatment it is not uncommon for the therapist to do at least half of the talking. Long silences are not considered to be therapeutically valid in most cases and the client will often be interrupted and redirected by the therapist in the interest of retaining focus. Between-session homework assignments are also used extensively in order to maximise therapeutic gain. As the name suggests, CBT between-session work targets both COGNITIVE and BEHAVIOURAL factors that perpetuate and maintain psychological disorders.

USING THE GLOSSARY

You may have noticed that some words are set in SMALL CAPITALS. This indicates that the glossary on page 109 carries a brief definition and explanation of the term. The SMALL CAPITALS can appear anywhere in the texts, quotes, subtitles or index.

1

THE ORIGINS OF COGNITIVE
BEHAVIOUR THERAPY

COGNITIVE behaviour therapy (CBT) has arisen from diverse
theoretical foundations. In this chapter we will discuss some of
the most relevant historical influences, which have informed and
shaped the development of CBT.

HISTORICAL CONTEXT

The field of psychology was dominated mid-century by
BEHAVIOURISM and PSYCHOANALYSIS. These two monolithic schools
had little in common. Behaviourists attached little importance to
the internal workings of an individual's mind and considered that
the external environment determined behaviour. Psychoanalysts,
on the other hand, considered the internal world of paramount
importance—but also largely unconscious and therefore hidden
from the individual. Therefore a trained analyst was needed to
guide the client toward insight. Neither of these schools placed
particular emphasis on commonplace, readily accessible thoughts
such as those which feature prominently in present day CBT.

However, from BEHAVIOURISM and PSYCHOANALYSIS emerged
several professionals with a burgeoning interest in the mediating
role of COGNITION between stimulus and response. Albert Ellis and
Aaron T. Beck developed their own psychotherapeutic approaches,
rational emotive therapy (RET) and COGNITIVE therapy (CT)
respectively. Donald Meichenbaum also developed his own
approach called self-instructional training (SIT). Both Ellis and Beck
came from PSYCHOANALYTICAL backgrounds, whilst Meichenbaum
started out as a behaviourist. All three of their approaches drew on
information gained from the behaviourist movement and early
behavioural experiments whilst giving COGNITION a central role.
COGNITIVE psychology became more widely accepted due to
validating research outcomes and changes within the BEHAVIOURIST
camp. By the 1970s COGNITIVE psychology was beginning to truly
flourish.

BEHAVIOURAL THERAPY INFLUENCES ON CBT

The historical influences of current day CBT stretch back to the beginning of the century and the famous work of Pavlov. Pavlov's work on CLASSICAL CONDITIONING (1927) provided roots for the development of behaviour therapy. Although Pavlov's experiments involved animal subjects, the assumption was that the principles derived from work with animals could be reasonably applied to humans. CLASSICAL CONDITIONING arose from Pavlov's well-known experiment often referred to as 'Pavlov's dogs'.

Because dogs produce saliva at the sight of food without any prior learning, food is an *unconditioned stimulus* and salivation is an *unconditioned response*. Pavlov experimented by sounding a bell immediately prior to presenting the dogs with food. The introduction of the bell had an interesting effect on the *unconditioned* response of salivation. After several repetitions of combining food with the sound of the bell, the dogs began to salivate upon hearing the bell. Hence the sound of the bell (*conditioned stimulus*), elicited salivation (*conditioned response*). Pavlov also investigated the effects of removing the unconditioned stimulus (food) when the bell was sounded. He found that over time the conditioned response (salivation) extinguished.

Around the same time, Thorndike and others were developing OPERANT CONDITIONING. Thorndike experimented using cats. The cats were placed in a box where the only means of escape came via the pulling of a loop. As the cats came to associate the pulling of the loop with escape, the time that elapsed between incarceration and escape diminished. OPERANT CONDITIONING holds that behaviour is largely determined by consequences. Hence the desirable result of escape reinforces the loop-pulling behaviour. As Pavlov discovered with his dogs and the erosion of their response to the bell, the removal of the reinforcing consequence (escape) eventually extinguished the cats' associated behaviour (loop-pulling).

These new learning models were later applied to experiments using human subjects. MALADAPTIVE BEHAVIOURS were created and subsequently eliminated using the learning principles of both

CLASSICAL and OPERANT CONDITIONING. Controversially, infants and children were frequently the subject of choice. Although seminal experiments such as that of Watson and Rayner (1920) would not make it past an ethics board today, their work provided much insight into the mechanics of human behaviour. Watson and Rayner worked with an infant known as 'Little Albert'. Little Albert was repeatedly shown a white rat whilst simultaneously subjected to a loud disturbing noise. After several repetitions of the appearance of a white rat accompanied by an unpleasant sound, the baby responded with fear at the sight of the rat alone. Little Albert's fear response quickly generalised to virtually any white object resembling a rat such as a swatch of white fur. From this experiment Watson and Rayner concluded that irrational fears or phobias were conditioned emotional responses to specific stimuli.

In the 1950s Burrhus Fredric Skinner and Joseph Wolpe were working independently on further advancing the learning theories borne out of Pavlov's and Thorndike's earlier contributions. Skinner invented an OPERANT CONDITIONING chamber commonly referred to as 'Skinner's box' when he was a Harvard graduate student in the 1930s. Skinner used animal subjects in the main and looked closely at rule-governed behaviour. He focused on the effects of positive reinforcement more than on punishment/ negative reinforcement. Skinner found that behaviours reinforced by a positive outcome (such as the delivery of food) were readily and consistently adopted by his animal subjects.

Joseph Wolpe introduced systematic desensitisation in 1958. He worked on the assumption that if ANXIETY responses could be legitimately considered conditioned responses (as asserted by Watson and Rayner) then a subject could theoretically be *de-conditioned*. Through habitual exposure to a conditioned stimulus *without* a negative reinforcer the conditioned fear response should eventually erode. Around the time of Wolpe, and in part due to his influence, behaviour therapy increasingly incorporated COGNITIVE VARIABLES into its treatment.

In the late 1960s and early 1970s Albert Bandura (Bandura, 1977a, b) laid down important stepping-stones toward an increased emphasis on COGNITIVE processes in behavioural therapy and clinical intervention. Bandura's social learning theory and behavioural modification approaches emphasised COGNITION as integral to behaviour acquisition and adjustment. In essence he disputed the traditional 'stimulus leads to response' paradigm affording the individual reciprocal influence on the environmental stimulus. Bandura was amongst the first to recognise COGNITIVE factors as pivotal to understanding learned behaviour. Social learning theory gave rise to COGNITIVE RECONCEPTUALISATION amongst several of Bandura's learning theorist contemporaries. This revolution in thinking provided a springboard for the manifestation of COGNITIVE theory and associated therapeutic orientations.

That said however, former psychoanalyst Albert Ellis had in fact been convinced that COGNITIVE VARIABLES mediated behaviour (based on his clinical experience) since as early as 1957. Aaron Beck began his own investigation into COGNITIVE aspects of depression in the early 1960s drawing somewhat on Ellis's theories. Yet it wasn't until the early 1970s that COGNITIVE therapeutic approaches gained true recognition. At this stage behavioural and COGNITIVE theory seem to have merged sufficiently to radicalise psychotherapeutic practice.

In addition to the professionals mentioned in this section, several others made significant contributions toward the advancement and development of COGNITIVE models. For an excellent review of the historical basis of COGNITIVE behavioural treatments, consult Dobson and Block, 1988. There are also two comprehensive chapters on the subject in Clark, Beck & Alford, 1999.

PHILOSOPHICAL UNDERPINNINGS OF CBT

Greek stoic philosophers devoted much thought to the SUBJECTIVE EXPERIENCE of reality. Much of stoical teaching emphasises the role of idiosyncratic meaning in defining human experience. Early philosophers such as Epictetus, Cicero, Seneca and Aurelius are well known for positing the notion that COGNITIVE VARIABLES mediate and determine emotional responses to events. Though they did not state these philosophies in such overtly scientific terms, the basic sentiment is represented in various sayings attributed to them, including 'man is not affected by events but by the view he takes of them' (Epictetus) and 'there is nothing either good or bad but thinking makes it so' *(Hamlet*, Shakespeare). The philosophical foundations of present-day CBT are also interlaced in the works of later philosophers such as Heidegger and Hegel.

COGNITIVE THERAPY INFLUENCES ON CBT

The term COGNITIVE behaviour therapy presently refers to a multitude of models accounting for human distress and a spectrum of associated interventions.

CBT places emphasis on the interaction and multidirectional relationship between COGNITIVE, behavioural and physiological realms. COGNITION and behaviour reciprocally influence one another to shape an individual's understanding and experience of his or her environment. Equally, emotions, environment and physiology influence COGNITION and behaviour. The CBT viewpoint of a highly reciprocal interactive system informs choice of intervention when dealing with psychological disturbance. Interventions are typically aimed at both dysfunctional COGNITION and behaviour. Thus CBT could simply be considered a hybrid between COGNITIVE and behavioural therapies. More accurately however, CBT has developed from a more complex amalgam of behaviour therapy and three distinct seminal schools of COGNITIVE therapy (Rachman & Wilson, 1980) as already mentioned in the introductory sections of this chapter. We now briefly describe these schools below:

The first school is Ellis's rational emotive therapy (RET). Rational emotive therapy posits that IRRATIONAL BELIEFS are at the core of emotional disturbance. In contrast, RATIONAL BELIEFS lead to functional emotional responses to adverse experiences. Characteristics of both types of beliefs are outlined below.

An ABC MODEL is used in RET. 'A' denotes an ACTIVATING EVENT that is mediated by beliefs (B) and leads to emotional, behavioural and COGNITIVE consequences at 'C'. Treatment involves aiding the client to identify IRRATIONAL BELIEFS, challenge and modify them. Belief modification is achieved through various interventions including: direct DISPUTATION of irrational thinking, behavioural testing of the validity and utility of beliefs, COGNITIVE RESTRUCTURING exercises and numerous homework tasks.

IRRATIONAL BELIEFS	*RATIONAL BELIEFS*
• Rigid and extreme	• Flexible and non-extreme
• Inconsistent with reality	• Consistent with reality
• Illogical	• Logical
• Unhelpful/impede problem solving	• Pragmatic/promote problem solving

The second of these influential schools of therapy is Beck's COGNITIVE Therapy (CT). Although Beck developed CT independently of RET, they share similar presumptions about the development and maintenance of psychological disturbance. Rational Emotive Therapy focuses primarily on the effect of IRRATIONAL BELIEFS on the appraisal of events as well as consequent emotions and behaviours. Faulty interpretations are considered a by-product of IRRATIONAL BELIEFS and therefore are typically reassessed only after belief change has taken place. COGNITIVE Therapy differs somewhat from RET in this regard, typically honing in on the distorted content of the appraisal itself. Distorted interpretations (or *inferences*) are challenged and modified using techniques similar to those employed in RET. Homework tasks are also a central feature of CT with the emphasis on achieving INFERENTIAL change.

Meichenbaum's Self-Instructional Training (SIT) is the third school of influence. Meichenbaum derived his model of therapy from Ellis's RET and from his own work using operant instruction with schizophrenic patients (Meichenbaum, 1969). Patients who were able to give themselves covert self-instruction were found to perform better at tasks than those who did not self-instruct. SIT is essentially a skills acquisition model that incorporates techniques such as modification of negative self-talk and the development of coping strategies and problem-solving skills. There are six stages of SIT treatment, namely:

1. Defining problems
2. Addressing identified problem areas
3. Attention-focusing training
4. Development of coping statements
5. COGNITIVE and behavioural error correction
6. Self-reinforcement

(See also *Stress Inoculation Training,* Meichenbaum, 1985)

There are many theoretical and technical consistencies amongst these three psychotherapeutic approaches, despite variations in application. Though developed independently, these three approaches have also influenced one another to a greater or lesser degree. Both RET, now known as Rational Emotive Behaviour Therapy and COGNITIVE Therapy in particular continue to wield considerable influence in the field of psychology. Beck's COGNITIVE theory and therapy of depression (which he began developing in the 1960s) is particularly well researched and is responsible for ground-breaking impact on COGNITIVE psychology and psychology in general.

CONCLUSION

Many various approaches to dealing with psychological disorders are currently practised and fall under the broad heading of CBT. Despite some fundamental variations in theory and practice all COGNITIVE approaches are unified by a number of basic assumptions namely:

1. COGNITIONS exist
2. COGNITIONS mediate psychological and behavioural problems
3. Mediating COGNITIVE factors can be examined and changed
4. Behavioural, emotional and COGNITIVE problems can be addressed via direct modification of dysfunctional mediating COGNITIONS.

The diagram below provides a visual representation of the historical antecedents of CBT as discussed in this chapter. For more in-depth information please investigate the recommended reading already mentioned in preceding sections and the references listed in this book's appendix.

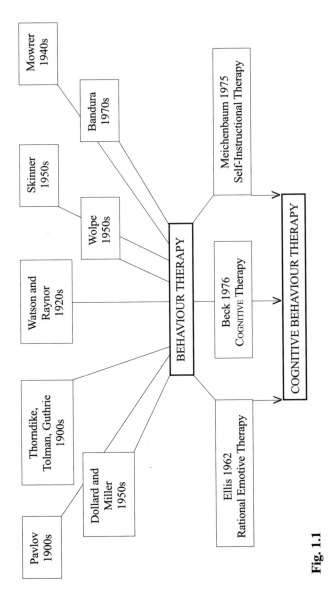

Fig. 1.1

2

THE THEORETICAL UNDERPINNINGS
OF COGNITIVE BEHAVIOUR THERAPY

THOUGHTS AND FEELINGS

The main reason people pursue counselling is because they are experiencing emotional problems such as depression, ANXIETY, anger or guilt. Rarely do clients arrive at the first session complaining about the way they *think*. Clients will typically describe their problems in one or more of the following ways:
- in terms of uncomfortable feelings that are impairing the client's daily functioning and/or enjoyment of life
- in terms of unsatisfactory life conditions such as work stress, sleep disturbance, relationship difficulties, financial worries and so on
- in terms of negative life events such as job loss, illness, relationship breakdown and traumatic incidents
- in terms of problematic behaviours such as addiction, procrastination, AVOIDANCE, social withdrawal, loss of temper etc.

However, dysfunctional thinking is at the very heart of emotional disturbance according to CBT theory. It is a commonly held assumption that other people's behaviour and undesirable external events *directly* cause us to feel negative emotions. Whilst it is true that when bad things happen people generally feel badly—CBT posits that these external conditions *contribute* to our negative emotions but are not solely or wholly responsible for causing emotional distress. Rather, according to CBT, how we interpret our experiences and appraise life events more profoundly affects our emotional responses than the event itself. A first-century AD philosopher called Epictetus summed up this connection between thought and emotion with his now famous adage, 'men are not disturbed by things but by the views which they take of them'.

Considering that any given individual's interpretations of what he or she experiences are by definition SUBJECTIVE, these are hypotheses or 'guesses' about reality, rather than solid 'facts' or evidence-based conclusions. Therefore they may be OBJECTIVELY correct or incorrect to varying degrees. Hence if an individual has persistent negative beliefs about himself and is given to particular styles of *thinking errors* (see Chapter 3), undue emotional disturbance is likely to follow negative events. Over time, such thinking will probably lead to emotional disorders such as depression. For example, a person may have a THINKING BIAS (or hold a false belief) that he is inadequate and worthless in an unfair and uncaring world. If a person truly believes such negative appraisals of himself and the world, it is easy to see how he may become depressed in the face of negative events, which he will construe as supporting evidence of his pre-existent belief system.

To illustrate, imagine that three men (alike in most fundamental respects) all fail a job interview. The first man feels very depressed about failing the interview, the second angry and the third disappointed. How do we account for the fact that in the face of the same event these three individuals manifest entirely different emotions?

It all begins to make sense when we consider that the first man believed 'failing this interview proves that I'm useless', the second held the belief 'I deserved that post and the company is stupid for not hiring me' and the third believed 'I really wanted that job and it's a real shame I wasn't offered it, but oh well'. Thus three different ways of thinking about the failed interview essentially produce three different ways of feeling.

THE ABC MODEL OF CBT

Albert Ellis, who founded RATIONAL Emotive Behaviour Therapy (REBT), put two distinct types of beliefs, *rational* and *irrational*, at point B in the ABC MODEL (see Fig. 2.1). According to Ellis, RATIONAL BELIEFS are flexible and non-extreme in nature whereas IRRATIONAL BELIEFS are extreme and rigid in nature. RATIONAL BELIEFS tend to produce healthy appropriate negative feelings in response to negative events, promote problem solving, self/other acceptance and healthy adjustment to undesired events or situations. Conversely, IRRATIONAL BELIEFS lead to unhealthy negative emotions, self/other downing, impaired problem solving and diminished adjustment in response to aversive events (Ellis, 1994). This concept is often referred to in CBT/REBT literature as the THOUGHT-FEELING LINK or the 'B-C connection'.

Returning to the example of the man who felt depressed after failing a job interview, we can conceptualise his depression using the ABC FORMAT as follows:

A. Failing a job interview (ACTIVATING EVENT)

B. I absolutely should have passed this interview (irrational demand)
   • It's awful that I didn't pass the interview (evaluation of 'awfulness')
   • Not passing the interview proves that I'm totally useless (self-denigration)

C. Depression (emotional consequence)
   • Withdraws from looking for potential work opportunities (behavioural consequence)
   • Ruminates on recent failure and focuses on imagined future failures to obtain work (COGNITIVE consequences)

We can also do an ABC on the second man's anger:

A. Failing a job interview (ACTIVATING EVENT)

B. I deserved the job and absolutely should have been offered it (irrational demand)
   • It's terrible that I wasn't offered the job (evaluation of 'awfulness')
   • Being refused this job just goes to show what idiots run that company (other-denigration)

C. Anger (emotional consequence)
   • Behaves defensively in next job interview (behavioural consequence)

- Fantasises about getting revenge on the company that refused him a job (COGNITIVE consequences)

Using the ABC FORMAT again we can see that the disappointed man held a rational preference to pass the interview and thus experienced a functional emotional response when he failed to do so:

A. Failing a job interview (ACTIVATING EVENT)

B. I really wanted to pass the job interview but there's no reason that I absolutely had to do so (rational preference)
  - It's bad that I didn't pass the interview but it's not the worst thing in the world (evaluation of 'badness')
  - Failing the interview means that I'm a fallible person but it doesn't mean that I'm useless (self-acceptance)

C. Disappointment (emotional consequence)
  - Continues to look for potential work opportunities (behavioural consequences)
  - Doesn't dwell on recent failure and is able to imagine obtaining work in the future (COGNITIVE consequences)

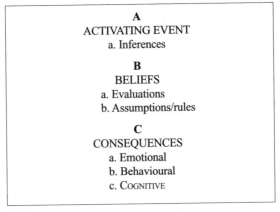

A
ACTIVATING EVENT
a. Inferences

B
BELIEFS
a. Evaluations
b. Assumptions/rules

C
CONSEQUENCES
a. Emotional
b. Behavioural
c. COGNITIVE

Fig. 2.1 The ABC MODEL

FUNCTIONAL AND DYSFUNCTIONAL NEGATIVE EMOTIONS

As already discussed in this chapter, CBT holds at its core the idea that our idiosyncratic interpretations and evaluations of our life experiences determine the *quality* of our negative emotional responses—healthy or unhealthy, ADAPTIVE or MALADAPTIVE. RATIONAL Emotive Behaviour Therapy (REBT) holds with a QUALITATIVE (two continua) versus QUANTITATIVE (single continuum) view of emotions. Unhealthy negative emotions are paired with a healthy alternative, for example, ANXIETY and concern. In REBT terms ANXIETY stems from an IRRATIONAL BELIEF and is therefore unhealthy, whereas concern stems from a RATIONAL BELIEF and is considered healthy.

Concern

| 1 | 2 | 3 | 4 | 5 | 6 | 7 | 8 | 9 | 10 |

Anxiety

| 1 | 2 | 3 | 4 | 5 | 6 | 7 | 8 | 9 | 10 |

Whilst both types of negative emotion can be experienced with varying degrees of intensity (as represented by the LIKERT SCALE) healthy emotions such as concern are associated with ADAPTIVE BEHAVIOURAL and COGNITIVE consequences whereas the unhealthy alternative (ANXIETY) will lead to MALADAPTIVE problematic consequences.

Most CBT therapists however, consider emotions to exist on a single continuum whereas milder emotions are generally accepted as healthier more functional alternatives to more extreme or intense feelings.

Concern   *Anxiety*

| 1 | 2 | 3 | 4 | 5 | 6 | 7 | 8 | 9 | 10 |

Perhaps the most significant benefit of Ellis's QUALITATIVE distinction between negative emotions is that it offers both therapists and clients a convenient readily understandable construct for discerning between functional emotional *distress* and inappropriate or dysfunctional emotional *disturbance/disorders.*

A fuller explanation of the REBT perspective on human emotion can be found in Dryden and Branch, 2008.

CHARACTERISTICS OF COGNITIVE BEHAVIOUR THERAPY

COGNITIVE therapy is usually thought of as a short-term therapy. It is true that CBT treatment is highly structured and incisive thus lending itself nicely to short-term intervention. Many clients will improve in as little as 13 sessions, although this is dependent on several factors such as the level of therapist competence, the severity and duration of the client's problem, environmental factors (unsatisfactory living circumstances, dysfunctional relationships, financial difficulties, etc, can impede therapeutic progress) and regular use of practical between-session assignments. Severe and chronic complaints may require long-term treatment and it is not unheard of for CBT treatment to span months, and in rarer cases, years. This is particularly likely when dealing with chronic depression, OBSESSIVE-COMPULSIVE DISORDER, personality disorders and other psychiatric conditions.

Whatever the duration of treatment, the characteristics of CBT remain the same. Below is a breakdown of defining key features of CBT.

Time limited

As already alluded to above, time limited does not necessarily equate to 'brief'. However, in early sessions treatment duration will be discussed. Following a full assessment the therapist will be able to give an informed estimation of how many sessions are likely to be required. Regular reviews are used to determine the rate of progress. Most CBT therapists will suggest an initial review after about six sessions.

Structured

There are clear beginning, middle and end stages of CBT treatment. In the early stage the client is introduced to the ABC MODEL, problems and goals are established and a conceptualisation formed. The bulk of the work takes place in the middle stage when the problem list is worked through. Toward the end of treatment the client is encouraged to take more control of sessions in preparation for acting as his own therapist post discharge. He is also urged to consolidate useful learning through review and consistent practice. Relapse prevention is also discussed.

Agenda based

Each session follows an agenda devised by client and therapist together. This helps keep focus within session and maximises the use of time.

Active-directive

The therapist is active and directive throughout treatment. Questions are asked, DIDACTIC TEACHING takes place, points are debated and suggestions are offered. In-session discussion is typically shared between client and therapist. This differs from non-directive forms of therapy where the client does the bulk of the talking.

Homework based

Between-session tasks are a major part of CBT treatment. Because most clients have one hourly session of therapy per week, it is important that they take new beliefs and behaviours acquired during sessions out into the real world. This progresses the therapeutic work from the intellectual to the experiential. The use of homework may well be the key factor that gives CBT its reputation for being efficient and long lasting.

Scientific

An experimental approach is taken to deal with client problems. Thoughts, attitudes, emotions and associated behaviours are delineated through the use of forms. Data is collected and examined, hypotheses are formulated, practical experiments devised and results evaluated. Additionally, CBT is well researched. Responsible therapists keep abreast of new findings, incorporating them into their existing practice as appropriate.

Collaborative

Client and therapist work side by side in an effort to resolve the former's difficulties. This promotes client independence and self-efficacy. Responsibility (and credit) for therapeutic gains are shared though ultimately progress is attributed to the client's hard work.

Explicit
CBT is a 'cards on the table' approach to dealing with psychological disturbance. Both client and therapist are equally aware of what is going on in sessions. Rather than forming silent interpretations of client belief systems, CBT therapists involve clients in open examination.

Psycho-educational
CBT therapists devote time to teaching the fundamentals of CBT and elicit questions, doubts or reservations the client may have about core theory. DIDACTIC TEACHING is part of the educative process but SOCRATIC QUESTIONING is also liberally employed. SOCRATIC QUESTIONING is also known as 'guided discovery' (Beck et al., 1979; Padesky, 1993; Persons, 1989). Rather than telling the client what to think, questions are asked that lead the client to discover answers for themselves. It is posited that self-generated solutions are more deeply experienced and enduring.

Problem focused
In the early sessions (if not in the initial session) clients are helped to devise a problem list. This may include emotional, behavioural and environmental difficulties that the client wants help resolving. The therapist helps to refine the problem list by placing problems in categories and then asks the client to rank them in order of importance. Generally problems that are most distressing or most interfere with day-to-day functioning are prioritised.

Goal focused
For each item on the problem list a goal is established. The goal will ideally include an emotional and a practical component. It is the therapist's job to ensure that goals are realistic and achievable. Goals will be reviewed regularly throughout treatment.

Ahistorical

CBT does not ignore the past as it has sometimes been accused. Past experiences and childhood events are explored in CBT but with the precise aim of understanding how they may be reinforcing current problems. Client history is therefore used to understand present difficulties and inform conceptualisation. Most of the therapeutic work is set in the present time. Unravelling and rehashing the past is not considered of fundamental therapeutic benefit nor are solutions considered to be hidden therein.

WHAT A SESSION OF CBT LOOKS LIKE

Not every session of CBT looks exactly the same. However, the session structure is clearly taught to trainees and most seasoned therapists will use an adaptation of it. Structure is invaluable for making the best use of the hour. It also helps the client to know what to expect from each session and therefore encourages them to arrive prepared. Bear in mind that though structured and focused, CBT therapists are not inflexible. In certain instances for example, the agenda may be suspended in favour of dealing with a recent client crisis. If a client is highly agitated, distressed or suicidal then these states take precedence and will be adequately addressed prior to returning to the typical agenda.

The following is a general guide to session format:
1. Greeting and mood check
2. Agenda setting
3. Homework and previous session review
4. Session objectives worked through
5. Homework setting
6. Feedback on session

Explanation of the six aspects of session format:
1. The client is greeted and asked about their current mood. Information gathered here may prompt agenda items.

2. Agenda items are noted. This may involve the therapist or client writing on a white board. Items may include recent

events, between-session practice, comments on previous session, troubleshooting for future tasks or events and emotional states. Homework review and feedback tend to be constant agenda items.

3. Learning outcomes from the previous session's homework are assessed. Obstacles to homework completion are investigated. If necessary previously assigned homework is modified.

4. Problems the client would like to address in session are defined and worked through. ABC forms may well be used to identify faulty thinking and/or behaviour. Additional techniques such as imagery, role-play and DISPUTATION are also frequently used. Clients are encouraged to transfer learning from previously resolved problems to their current difficulties.

5. Based on session content new homework is devised. Both client and therapist work to devise homework that is well suited to the client's problems. Opportunities to practise in-session learning and execute between-session tasks are identified. Often specific times for doing homework are scheduled into the client's week. This helps to ensure that tasks are carried out and not left to the last minute.

6. The client is invited to give feedback on their experience of the session and ask questions. Any important issues raised will be added to the following session's agenda if time does not allow for immediate discussion.

In the following chapters we will look more closely at CBT theory and interventions.

3

COGNITION

COGNITION is the 'C' in CBT. By the Oxford American dictionary definition the term means:

> COGNITION (noun) the mental action or process of acquiring knowledge and understanding through thought, experience, and the senses.
>
> • a result of this; a perception, sensation, notion, or intuition.

In CBT the emphasis is on enhancing or developing ADAPTIVE COGNITION that helps the client adjust to altered circumstances, overcome aversive experiences and act in a constructive, goal-oriented manner. People with healthy beliefs (COGNITIONS) tend to experience fewer episodes of psychological disturbance and therefore are less likely to seek out therapy. Because of this point, much of CBT treatment focuses on eliciting and restructuring MALADAPTIVE goal-impeding thinking. In this chapter we will explain the different categories of COGNITION that CBT recognises.

People are highly idiosyncratic with regard to the beliefs they hold and how they interpret the world around them. However, CBT has investigated the ways people think to such an extent that recurrent themes have been identified. Below is a list of twelve THINKING BIASES (Burns, 1990) frequently demonstrated by people suffering from emotional problems such as depression and ANXIETY.

COGNITIVE DISTORTIONS

1. All or nothing thinking
Thinking in extremes, which often leads to extreme emotional and behavioural responses. For example, a situation is either altogether bad or wholly good with no middle ground taken into account. Human experiences are rarely so stark.

2. Over-generalisation

Also referred to as the 'part-whole error' this involves forming global evaluations on the basis of one or more aspects of oneself or a situation. For example a woman concludes that she is a terrible mother on the basis of losing patience with her child on one or a few occasions.

3. Mental filtering

An information-processing bias in which one only acknowledges information that fits with a pre-existent belief. For example one believes one is unlovable and therefore overlooks evidence to the contrary. The strongly held negative self-belief acts as a filter for one's experiences.

4. Mind reading

The tendency to assume that one knows what others are thinking about him or some aspect of his performance. Rather than acknowledging that it is impossible to know for certain the content of another individual's mind, one believes that their assumptions (usually negative) are correct.

5. Labelling

Evaluating one's whole self on the basis of one or more characteristics, actions or thoughts is known as 'labelling'. It is similar to over-generalisation, or the 'part-whole' error, because the whole is given an absolute label according to one or more of its components. For example labelling yourself a 'loser' on the basis of having failed at an important task.

6. Fortune telling

Making predictions (usually negative) about the future. This often results in AVOIDANCE and procrastination. Continually predicting negative outcomes can become a self-fulfilling prophecy. For example, a depressed woman predicts that she will not enjoy going out with friends and thus avoids doing so. She also predicts that she will be unable to cope with daily chores and thus increases the likelihood of becoming overwhelmed should she make a start.

7. Emotional reasoning

Using strong emotions as reliable indicators of reality. This can be problematic as one then ceases to seek out alternative information that may provide a more accurate account of a situation. For example, someone with agoraphobia assumes that because they feel so intensely anxious when in unfamiliar surroundings that there must be a real and present danger.

8. Personalisation

Placing one's self at the centre of negative events. Rather than taking into account other contributing factors, personal responsibility for an undesirable outcome is assumed. For example a close friend appears sad and withdrawn and one automatically assumes one has caused offence in some way.

9. Magnification and minimisation

An ATTENTIONAL BIAS where an individual focuses on negative features of themselves or a situation and magnifies their severity. Conversely positive features are ignored or minimised. For example, during a presentation an individual stumbles over a few words. Afterward, although the remainder of his performance was adequate, he ruminates on this blunder and fails to view it within the context of the overall presentation.

10. Demanding

Applying rigid rules to one's self, others and the world. These unrelenting rules typically start off as strong preferences and are transmuted into 'should', 'must' and 'have to' imperatives. They leave no room for deviation or error and when unmet result in emotional disturbance. For example, because I strongly *prefer* to be approved of by my parents I therefore *must* have their approval at all times.

11. Disqualifying the positive

An information processing bias similar to mental filtering. The distinction is that in this case information that contradicts a strongly held negative belief (such as being unlovable) is disqualified or discounted. Information may also be transmuted to fit with the pre-existent belief. For example, someone who believes himself to be unlovable receives a smile from a stranger and this is twisted into meaning that he is being ridiculed.

12. Jumping to conclusions
Leaping immediately to a negative interpretation of an event despite the absence of evidence to support this. For example a woman's husband is late home and she interprets this to mean 'he's had a car crash'.

Everyone makes thinking errors occasionally. Some you probably make more often than others. COGNITIVE distortions are commonplace and do not indicate psychological or emotional disturbance. They do however feature largely in skewing interpretations of individual experience and hence are clinically informative.

NEGATIVE AUTOMATIC THOUGHTS (NATS)

These are thoughts that just seem to pop into one's head in certain situations. Frequently these thoughts take the form of truncated sentences such as 'No one likes me'. Typically NATS are a by-product of the COGNITIVE DISTORTIONS listed above and are AFFECT LADEN. Automatic thoughts most related to an individual's emotional experience are most therapeutically relevant and are targeted in CBT treatment (Padesky & Greenberger, 1995).

Because they are seemingly spontaneous and readily accessible to the client, NATS are described as 'automatic'. More accurately however, NATS arise when assumptions and CORE BELIEFS, which the client may be far less aware of, are triggered.

Illustrative example: Monica was chubby as a child. She grew up being teased about her weight by peers and told by family how 'pretty she would be if only she wasn't so fat'. Her family placed a lot of importance on physical appearance and personal presentation. Because Monica was not able to please her family

> with her looks, she often sensed their disappointment and disapproval. Monica developed an image of herself as fundamentally defective and of other people as critical and hurtful. Although Monica has maintained a 'normal' weight as an adult, she remains extremely sensitive to comments about her appearance and is very suspicious of others' intentions when they make any mention of her figure or looks in general. Monica will even readily interpret blatant compliments as cloaked criticism.

We can see how the negative beliefs that Monica developed about herself and others in her early life continue to dog her in her adult life.

We can further understand from Monica's example that CORE BELIEFS (see section below) such as 'I'm defective' skew one's interpretation of actual events at 'A' and influence the evaluation assigned to these events at 'B' in the ABC MODEL.

ASSUMPTIONS

Assumptions are like contingency plans that individuals devise to compensate for their negative CORE BELIEFS. They are another layer of rules that often take the form of 'if–then' statements. For example 'If I can get others to like me then I can view myself as somewhat worthwhile'. On the other side of the coin, they also act to reinforce the negative CORE BELIEF. For example 'If I am rejected then it proves that I am worthless'.

CORE BELIEFS

Long-held enduring beliefs about one's self, other people and the world/life are called CORE BELIEFS or CORE SCHEMATA. They comprise the deepest level of COGNITION and hence are not at the forefront of people's minds as are assumptions and automatic thoughts. They are, however, hardwired into an individual's way of thinking and determine how they make sense of their experiences. CORE BELIEFS are absolute rigid rules, which give rise to assumptions and automatic thoughts. They are typically experienced as facts rather than as personal beliefs. Maladaptive or unhealthy CORE BELIEFS often lead to emotional and psychological problems impeding goal attainment. Below is an example of the three types of unhealthy CORE BELIEFS:

Self: I'm worthless

Others: People are cruel

World/Life: Life is perilous

CORE BELIEFS tend to be formed in childhood and early adult life. Frequently they are formed in response to early experiences. Thus CORE BELIEFS may well 'fit' with an individual's early understanding of themselves and their world. Additionally they may have served a functional purpose at one time. For example, assume you had neglectful and abusive parents plus you were the target of frequent criticism from your teachers. Now imagine that you also found it difficult to make friends and were subjected to bullying at school. It makes sense that you might conclude (erroneously) that you're worthless. Certainly that message has been consistently received. Your survival instincts may also lead you to conclude that other people are cruel and best treated with suspicion. A further conclusion may be that life itself is harsh and unyielding.

Because CORE BELIEFS are—just as the name implies—at the very core of our understanding of ourselves, they are notoriously difficult to shift. An individual will live their life according to the SUBJECTIVE truth of these beliefs. Experiential evidence that contradicts CORE BELIEFS will be ignored, overlooked and misinterpreted. Padesky (1993) equates this information-processing bias with holding a prejudice. Only information consistent with the pre-existent belief system is acknowledged. As a result, CORE SCHEMATA are rarely challenged, re-evaluated or updated by the client. CBT aims to assist clients in reassessing the validity of their unhealthy CORE BELIEFS and to form healthy alternatives.

It is also useful to consider the effects each type of belief (self, other and world) have on one another. To understand more fully an individual's emotional problems it helps to have a full picture of all three types of CORE BELIEFS they hold. CORE BELIEFS are mutually influential. If a client believes himself to be weak, others to be malicious and the world unfriendly, it is hardly surprising that he feels helpless and depressed.

Fig. 3.1

As Fig. 3.2 illustrates, we can conceptualise CORE SCHEMATA as the bull's eye of the COGNITIVE dartboard with subsequent thoughts radiating from them.

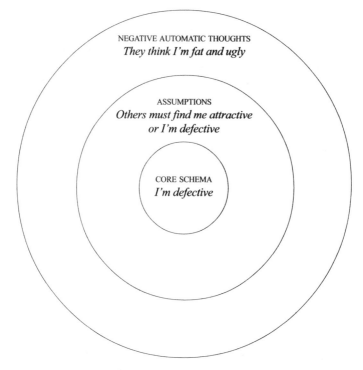

Fig. 3.2

Interaction

The interaction between these three sets of beliefs provides the basis of the CBT conceptual model. Staying with the example of Monica, we can observe how her CORE BELIEFS influence her interpretation of events, give rise to NATS, assumptions and problematic emotional/behavioural responses.

CORE BELIEF
I'm defective

ASSUMPTION
If others find me unattractive then I am defective

TRIGGER EVENT
Co-worker comments that Monica looks like she's lost weight

NEGATIVE AUTOMATIC THOUGHT
'He thinks I'm fat, ugly and that I need to lose weight'

EMOTIONAL RESPONSE
Shame and depression

BEHAVIOURAL RESPONSE
Avoids eating in front of co-worker
Gives co-worker the cold shoulder
Resolves to go on a crash diet

This is a typical example of how unhealthy CORE SCHEMATA are maintained and reinforced through the misinterpretation of contradictory, and the collection of confirming, information. Also note that Monica's ego-defensive actions (borne of her feelings of shame and depression) are likely to alienate her co-worker. Her co-worker may be inclined to withdraw from Monica, which she may interpret as further rejection and proof of her belief that she is defective. A vicious cycle perpetuates. Since CORE SCHEMATA are deeply entrenched and almost impervious to DISPUTATION (certainly in the early stages of CBT treatment) intervention is often first directed toward challenging assumptions and re-evaluating interpretations of events. Behavioural responses are also examined for their utility and alternatives are collaboratively devised to bring about more favourable results. Interventions aimed at these areas are often more readily palatable to clients and serve to obliquely erode negative CORE BELIEFS.

A comprehensive discussion of the techniques used to challenge and restructure negative beliefs like Monica's is unfortunately beyond the scope of this book. Basic interventions are described in Chapter 6 and further recommended reading is included in the appendix. Later we will discuss various methods of identifying client beliefs.

4

COGNITIVE BEHAVIOUR THERAPY
AND THE THERAPEUTIC ALLIANCE

Several psychotherapeutic approaches, which preceded the advent of CBT, regard the relationship between client and therapist as the bedrock of therapeutic change.

It is a common criticism that CBT undervalues or even neglects the CORE CONDITIONS as outlined by Rogers (1957). Whilst it is true that CBT holds a specific stance on the THERAPEUTIC ALLIANCE that is at variance with other types of therapy, it is inaccurate to say that CBT fails to recognise the importance of the CORE CONDITIONS. In fact many of the ALLIANCE CONCEPTS outlined in PSYCHOANALYTICAL and humanistic approaches such as EMPATHY, warmth, CONGRUENCE, UNCONDITIONAL POSITIVE REGARD, TRANSFERENCE and COUNTER-TRANSFERENCE are represented in CBT theory and readily translatable into CBT practice (Safran & Segal, 1990; Wills & Sanders, 1997).

Perhaps the most significant point of divergence between Rogerian and CBT is that Rogers considered the CORE CONDITIONS to be *both* necessary and sufficient for therapeutic change to occur, whilst CBT recognises the conditions as desirable and necessary but not sufficient to bring about client change (Beck et al, 1979).

ROGERS' CORE CONDITIONS

EMPATHY

CBT holds accurate EMPATHY to be extremely important in order for therapy to be effective. Like other therapeutic approaches, CBT recognises that the client needs to not only *feel* understood but to actually *be* understood. CBT pays close attention to the behaviours and behavioural tendencies associated with specific emotions. Thus the CBT therapist can readily convey understanding of how the client feels by referring to how they may be acting or be inclined to act. Additionally, because certain beliefs and thoughts are thematically consistent with specific emotions, CBT therapists are able to convey both affective EMPATHY and philosophical EMPATHY. In brief, the therapist demonstrates understanding of the emotions experienced by the client and of the thoughts which give rise to those feelings.

Warmth

A non-judgemental approachable demeanour is desirable in a CBT therapist. Conveying a degree of professional warmth may be particularly useful with depressed or suicidal clients and those with very poor self-opinion. By 'professional warmth' we mean imparting to your client a sense of being liked and respected whilst maintaining clear boundaries of a professional relationship.

There are contraindications to be considered regarding warmth toward clients. Clients who lack self-efficacy can become overly dependent on a warm therapist. Also, negative CORE BELIEFS that spur the client to seek approval from others can be inadvertently reinforced through therapist warmth.

There are also potential confounding issues for the therapist. CBT therapists who are overly warm toward their clients may find it more difficult to be active-directive in treatment. It may be difficult for the therapist to establish his role as 'expert' in early treatment if he is overly focused on being warm.

Sometimes it can be challenging for the therapist to feel warmth toward a client who does not engender such feelings. In this case forcing the matter will almost certainly smack of insincerity. Behaving in a polite interested manner and seeking supervision is recommended in this instance.

UNCONDITIONAL POSITIVE REGARD

Rather than prizing each client in the Rogerian sense (Rogers, 1957) CBT therapists practise *acceptance* toward their clients. Acceptance involves recognising the intrinsic value of each client whilst acknowledging him or her as a fallible human being. The client is treated with respect and caring regardless of any mistakes or misdeeds. This is not to say that the CBT therapist will gloss over self-destructive (or other-destructive) behaviours the client may disclose. Conversely, CBT focuses on helping clients to understand and modify behaviours and thoughts that interfere with reaching therapeutic goals. Whilst the client's faulty ways of *thinking and acting* will be directly evaluated and challenged, this is done without judging the client as a *whole person*. It takes skill to be able to confront a client's maladaptive beliefs and coping strategies without leading them to infer personal disapproval. Because CBT is an explicit therapy, the practitioner will often devote time to socialising clients to the model. Educating clients about what they can expect to happen in sessions, with regard to direct challenges, can reduce the risk of clients feeling negatively judged.

CONGRUENCE and genuineness

These conditions are perhaps most obviously represented within the context of collaboration as discussed in the following section.

Suffice it to say that CBT does not operate any hidden agendas. The client is privy to therapist musings about what may be perpetuating his problems. Additionally, any early experiences that may have contributed to the formation of dysfunctional beliefs are discussed openly between client and therapist. The therapist takes the role of authoritative expert in the field of psychology and is willing to share knowledge with the client. The client is an expert of his own experiences and hence plays a vital role in providing the information necessary for therapeutic work to commence.

Skilled CBT therapists are consistent in how they respond to their clients. They exhibit genuine reactions but are appropriately sensitive to their potential effect on the client. CBT discourages therapist dishonesty and insincerity. Therefore therapists will ideally avoid offering platitudes, false praise or empty compliments. In these ways CBT therapists are open, genuine and congruent.

COLLABORATION

The CBT therapist and client working alongside one another in a joint endeavour to resolve the latter's difficulties is known as COLLABORATIVE EMPIRICISM. Basically this term refers to the working relationship whereby the client provides the therapist with information and the therapist uses her expertise to help the client challenge unhelpful beliefs and behaviour. Initially, the therapist will take a lead role in structuring sessions and as therapy progresses the client will be encouraged to take the lead more often. This shift in responsibility for leading treatment is in keeping with the CBT objective of assisting clients to become their own therapists.

Because client and therapist are working together, any hypotheses made by the therapist are offered to the client for confirmation, disconfirmation or adjustment. Additionally, rather than forming silent interpretations, the therapist will explore her client's emotions, thoughts and behaviours overtly. In addition to being a structured goal-directed treatment, CBT acknowledges that a good working alliance promotes client trust thereby increasing compliance. Because between-session assignments are an integral part of CBT treatment, the client needs to feel that the therapist is genuinely interested in his progress and understands his problems. Otherwise the client is less likely to carry out goal-directed tasks, which are often challenging and uncomfortable as 'homework'.

USE OF HUMOUR

Therapy can be a serious business. Certainly the suffering of those with psychological and emotional disorders is no laughing matter. That said, Albert Ellis, founder of RATIONAL Emotive Behaviour Therapy (REBT), purports that individuals with neurotic disorders frequently fall prey to taking themselves and certain life events *overly* seriously (Dryden & Branch, 2008). The appropriate use of humour may help strengthen the alliance, normalise symptoms and can help to humanise the therapist. When used therapeutically, humour can also encourage the client to take a more light-hearted view of faulty thinking and self-defeating behaviours. Rather than berate himself for experiencing emotional problems, the judicial use of humour encourages the client to laugh at *aspects* of his thinking and actions whilst simultaneously holding an accepting and compassionate attitude toward himself.

We emphasise that it is not appropriate for the therapist to make jokes at the client's expense or to use humour to ease their own personal discomfort within session. As with any intervention, humour should be employed for the potential benefit it may hold for the client.

Caution and forethought are recommended when using humour. Some clients may welcome a joke or two but covertly use it to avoid discussing painful emotions or to deflect the therapist from more serious dimensions of treatment. Clients with CORE BELIEFS about needing to be liked and approved of may use humour as a way of 'winning over' the therapist. It is worthwhile paying close attention to signs that your client is making it his job to keep you entertained in sessions.

THERAPIST SELF-DISCLOSURE

Unlike other schools of psychotherapy, CBT supports the prudent use of therapist self-disclosure. When patients ask the therapist questions, they will frequently benefit from an honest and measured answer. After all, CBT is a collaborative process and hence it follows that the exchange of information is, to a degree, two-way. Certainly questions pertaining to the therapist's training or experience of working with a specific problem area are well within the client's right to ask. CBT therapists will answer such questions honestly and responsibly.

Clients may also pose a host of different questions to the therapist particularly once it has been established that it is acceptable to do so. Some of these questions may be inconsequential and asked out of politeness or common curiosity such as 'are you going on holiday this summer?' or 'did you have a nice weekend?' With these types of questions there is little risk to consider and brief polite responses will normally suffice. Other times the client may ask more personal questions based on whatever is being discussed in session. Forthright questions such as 'are you divorced?' and more obliquely phrased ones 'I don't know, perhaps you've been through a divorce yourself ...' require thoughtful handling. The general rule is to answer questions if doing so is likely to be helpful, *or at least not harmful*, for the client. Questions of a personal nature can be awkward for therapists. Some therapists are able to answer such enquiries and maintain a professional stance. Others may choose not to answer but provide the client with a reasonable explanation for their refusal.

In certain instances the therapist may also choose to disclose unsolicited information. Telling anecdotes, using metaphors and sharing stories related to your client's situation might benefit the alliance, instil hope of recovery or provide a useful template for understanding problems.

It is always important to assess the possible effect of sharing personal information with your client. Ask yourself:
- How is my client likely to make sense of this information?
- Will giving this information impact negatively on the THERAPEUTIC ALLIANCE?
- Will my client be able to use this information constructively?

TRANSFERENCE AND COUNTER-TRANSFERENCE

These concepts comprise much of analytical therapeutic approaches. Whilst CBT does not incorporate TRANSFERENCE as a key aspect of therapeutic intervention, it does acknowledge the role it plays in the therapeutic relationship. Just as every client brings to session their own belief systems, so do therapists.

Firstly the client may wittingly or unwittingly attempt to elicit responses from the therapist that are in keeping with their CORE SCHEMATA. In this sense the client engages in 'schema maintenance' (Young, Klosko & Weishaar, 2003), which draws a parallel with TRANSFERENCE. In essence the client provokes the type of reaction he or she expects to receive from others. Unlike traditional psychoanalysts, the CBT practitioner may well discuss this phenomenon openly with the client when it is deemed timely and appropriate.

Secondly, therapist reactions to the client, and/or the material shared, are considered within the context of the therapist's idiosyncratic belief system. Hence the therapist is responsible for his own emotional responses to the client. This notion is not entirely dissimilar to COUNTER-TRANSFERENCE. To clarify, client and therapist schemata can often bump up against one another and produce complex nuances in the alliance. The CBT therapist's personal reactions to the client will be discussed and conceptualised, as per the ABC MODEL, in supervision.

IN CONCLUSION

Because of its scientific basis and structured approach, CBT can be difficult to master whilst adhering to the CORE CONDITIONS. Students and trainees often seem to be so focused on getting the treatment sequence correct that adherence to the CORE CONDITIONS temporarily seems to fly out of the consulting room window. Maintaining the CORE CONDITIONS whilst conducting competent CBT takes practice and is an issue frequently addressed in trainee supervision.

Despite comparatively sparse mention of the CORE CONDITIONS in much of CBT literature, they are a key feature of CBT's overall approach. Gilbert and Leahy (2007) have helped fill this gap through their writings on the role of the therapeutic relationship in CBT. Rather than being guilty of neglecting or rejecting the importance of the THERAPEUTIC ALLIANCE, perhaps it is more accurate to say that CBT has fallen foul of taking it for granted. CBT may benefit from further disseminating its unique viewpoint on the conditions that favourably influence therapeutic change. Fortunately more research is currently focused on this area and hopefully will help to dispel accusations of CBT as insensitive to the relationship between therapist and client.

5

CASE CONCEPTUALISATION

BASIC CONCEPTUALISATION

Basic CASE CONCEPTUALISATION is a means of understanding the client's presenting problems. Beck's COGNITIVE model of emotional disorders (Beck, Emery & Greenberg, 1985) is commonly applied to conceptualisation. As already described in previous chapters, the COGNITIVE model assumes that thoughts, feelings and behaviours are interrelated and mutually reinforcing. Therefore a simple conceptualisation focuses on the vicious cycle that develops between these areas. See the diagram below by way of example.

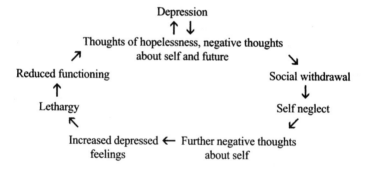

Padesky and Mooney (1990) developed a generic model sometimes referred to as the 'hot cross bun' because of its appearance (see Fig. 5.1 below).

This model pulls together environmental, COGNITIVE, behavioural and biological factors showing how these areas impact on one another. It provides a useful simple overview that can help clients to see their problems as multi-dimensional. As Wills and Sanders (1997) point out, this model can be very useful for clients who attribute their difficulties wholly to biological and medical factors. Because it includes all aspects of the client's functioning it serves as a palatable introduction to a psychological perspective on human disturbance.

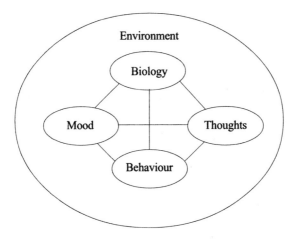

Fig. 5.1 Hot Cross Bun/Generic Model

Fig. 5.2 Simple Vicious Flower

Another simple but effective conceptualisation tool is the vicious flower (Hackman, 1998). This model exhibits how the client's main problem produces symptoms (thoughts and behaviours), which in turn further reinforce and maintain the primary problem. This model is of particular use when treating ANXIETY disorders because of the tendency for suffers to employ AVOIDANCE strategies that prevent them from confronting their fears. A further advantage of the vicious flower is that as many petals as necessary can be added on.

The vicious flower has been developed to give a fuller view of problem causation and maintenance.

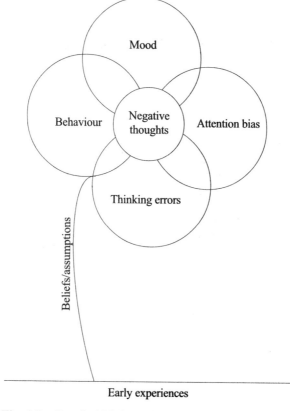

Early experiences

Fig. 5.3   Detailed Vicious Flower

DETAILED CONCEPTUALISATION

A simple conceptualisation is sufficient to be getting on with. Generally represented in ABC FORMAT, it serves to identify TRIGGER EVENTS (A); thoughts, evaluations and assumptions (B); plus emotional, behavioural and COGNITIVE responses (C). As problems are worked through, themes may begin to emerge which indicate the presence of CORE SCHEMATA.

Therefore as therapy progresses, and more information about the client is gathered, conceptualisation develops more fully. The CBT therapist keeps an eye on underlying mechanisms that may be maintaining problems and considers historical experiences that may have contributed to the formation of unhelpful CORE BELIEFS. As always, the development of a detailed conceptualisation includes both client and therapist input.

The process of deepening and refining the overall picture of the client's problems can help to strengthen client understanding of how they have arrived where they are today. This increased insight may help the client to better recognise potential points for intervention. It also provides a bridge between past and present experiences (Wills & Sanders, 1997).

Illustrative example: Gavin suffers from depression and ANXIETY. He often worries that he's about to be fired from his job despite the fact that there has never been any mention of this in appraisals. He keeps to himself and feels anxious in social situations because he worries a lot about whether or not others like him. Generally Gavin assumes that others find him uninteresting at best. Gavin remains single, not out of choice but because he refuses to approach females for fear of being rejected. Some of Gavin's early experiences were quite negative. His parents were rather unapproachable and he was never able to gain his father's approval. As a shy boy, Gavin was never popular at school and was often teased and ostracised by his peers.

Using the information included in this example we can build a comprehensive conceptualisation of Gavin's current problems of depression and ANXIETY.

Presenting problems
Depression
Social anxiety and general worry
Unable to find a romantic partner

Significant early/childhood experiences
Bullied in primary school, parents unsupportive
Critical father, 'nothing I did was ever good enough'
First love laughed at him when he asked her out on a date

Environmental factors
Living alone (rented flat)
Minimal contact with family
Secure employment

CORE BELIEFS
Self: I'm inadequate
Others: Others are superior to me
World: Life favours the strong

Assumptions/rules
If I avoid getting close to people then I can stay safe
If others like me then I'm OK (because my inadequacy is
    hidden)
I must always work hard to make up for my basic inadequacy

ACTIVATING EVENTS
Being criticised
Seeming to be left out of conversations
Interpersonal confrontation

Compensatory strategies
Avoids forging friendships/romantic relationships
Assumes others are untrustworthy until proven otherwise
Backs down in confrontations
Works hard to please others and avoid criticism

The conceptualisation format above has been adapted from
Judith Beck (1995).

CONSIDERATIONS WHEN FORMING A CONCEPTUALISATION

A conceptualisation is like a road map that is intended to help both client and therapist arrive at a particular destination. It helps therapist and client to tackle problems in a sensible order thus directing treatment toward therapeutic goals. A well-constructed problem formulation can prove invaluable as it makes clear the most advantageous areas to target interventions and provides information about which techniques are most likely to be of benefit. Trainees and experienced therapists alike find that presenting CASE CONCEPTUALISATIONS helps them to make good use of clinical supervision.

It is important to remember however, that every therapist brings their own clinical experience and theoretical knowledge to their conceptualisation. Clients are idiosyncratic individuals despite the fact that their emotional disturbances may be very well documented and familiar to the therapist. Hence it cannot be stressed enough that the client should be included in the process of building a conceptualisation. Not every client will fit as neatly into a pre-existing model as may be expected. It pays to listen closely to your client's description of how they experience difficulties and to avoid concluding that they are a 'textbook' case. The client should ideally be given regular opportunities to disagree with, subtly adjust or entirely reject the formulation. Often clients are reluctant to voice objections to the therapist for a host of reasons and need to be directly encouraged to do so. It is the therapist's task to form a good working alliance with their clients and to be clear that CBT is a two-person therapy. The therapist may be the expert in CBT but that does not mean he or she is always right. Above all, CBT therapists need to be flexible and modify conceptualisations as new information emerges throughout treatment.

6

COGNITIVE RESTRUCTURING
TECHNIQUES

The process of assessment in CBT begins to socialise the client to the CBT model. Asking clients to identify ways of thinking, in relation to emotional and practical problems, introduces the principle of THOUGHT–FEELING INTERACTION. Sometimes just asking the client to be more mindful of his thoughts, beliefs and personal rules for living can be enough to kick start COGNITIVE modification. However, to effect meaningful long-lasting change to entrenched personal schema, much diligent practice is required. COGNITIVE RESTRUCTURING takes place at any level of COGNITION although changes are more philosophically profound and pervasive when they occur at core schema level.

For every negative schema challenged and eroded, a healthy alternative schema needs to be developed and strengthened. The same applies for interpretations, NEGATIVE AUTOMATIC THOUGHTS (NATS) and assumptions. See examples below:

CORE BELIEF (negative): *I'm worthless*
Healthy alternative: *I have personal worth*

Assumption (negative): *If I can impress others then I can have some sense of worth*
Healthy alternative: *My worth is consistent whether I impress others or not*

NAT: *Everyone at work thinks I'm useless*
Healthy alternative: It's not possible to know what others think of me, I'm not a mind-reader

Interpretation (negative): *My boss was grumpy this morning because I somehow offended him*
Healthy alternative: *There are any number of possible reasons for my boss being grumpy, it may be nothing to do with me*

In this chapter we will look at some of the more common methods of challenging dysfunctional thoughts and strengthening healthy alternative ways of thinking.

In order to begin work on restructuring thoughts the client first needs to be prepared to do a few things:

1. Understand and accept the psychological component of his problems. In short, thoughts and feelings are closely linked, therefore dysfunctional thinking leads to emotional disturbance.

2. Become more aware of his thinking in general and specifically in relation to his identified problems.

3. Catch and record NEGATIVE AUTOMATIC THOUGHTS, thinking distortions and assumptions in TRIGGER situations.

4. Develop a willingness to be sceptical about the validity of his thoughts and beliefs.

It is the therapist's task to help the client meet the above points. Teaching examples, metaphors, DIDACTIC explanation, bibliotherapy and SOCRATIC QUESTIONING may all be used to achieve this aim.

DAILY THOUGHT RECORDS

The Daily Thought Record (DTR) is perhaps one of the most commonly used forms in early sessions of CBT. It has its uses throughout treatment but is probably most useful when clients are just beginning to relate their thoughts to their emotions. Many different versions of the thought record exist. Some are simpler and omit headings included on the traditional DTR. The traditional DTR (see Fig. 6.1) has the benefit of providing space to identify TRIGGER situations, NEGATIVE AUTOMATIC THOUGHTS, thinking errors, healthy alternative thoughts and resulting emotions all on one page. (Unfortunately this comprehensive format leaves rather little space for the client to write in, which is a drawback.) The DTR is generally given to the client to use between sessions and bring back to the therapist for collaborative review.

Date	EMOTION(S) What do you feel? How bad is it? (0–100)	SITUATION What were you doing? Where were you?	AUTOMATIC THOUGHTS What exactly were your thoughts? How far did you believe each of them? (0–100)	THINKING ERRORS I AM ENGAGING IN	RATIONAL RESPONSE What are your rational answers to the automatic thoughts? How much do you believe each of them? (0–100)	OUTCOME RE-RATE MOOD NOW (0–100%) How much do you believe original thoughts? (0–100). What can you do now?

Fig. 6.1 Daily Thought Record

ABC FORMS

Like the Daily Thought Record, many different versions of the ABC form are used. They can be used as an assessment tool or in lieu of a DTR. The form itself is rather self-explanatory. It is used to break down the client's problem into three distinct components: a definite TRIGGER, thought and emotion. CBT therapists often give their clients ABC forms to use between sessions and will go over them in the next session. A single form is used for each specific example of a target problem.

ABC Form

A (ACTIVATING EVENT)
What happened?

Where were you?

When was it?

B (BELIEFS)
What thoughts did you have about the event?

C (CONSEQUENCES)
Emotional
How did you feel?

What emotion did you experience?

Behavioural
What did you do?

What did you feel inclined to do?

Fig. 6.2 ABC Form

RECORDING CHALLENGES TO NEGATIVE THINKING

Disputing negative beliefs in session is extremely useful. Because clients believe so firmly in their view of things, it is frequently difficult for them to generate convincing arguments against their negative thoughts. For this reason the CBT therapist will typically do the bulk of the disputing in the first instance. Once the client has grasped the process he is encouraged to form his own disputes.

The purpose of challenging negative thoughts is (rather obviously) to promote psychological health through the formation of more adaptive belief systems. By developing arguments 'for' a new belief and 'against' an old one, the client begins to truly embrace positive change. These arguments then need to be repeated by the client between sessions. Simply telling the client to think *x* instead of *y* does not bring about profound belief change. Rather the therapist shows the client how to use challenges to increase his conviction in new ways of thinking. The following section describes different types of questions both client and therapist can use to this end. Recording challenges either by writing them down or taping the therapy session helps the client to remember useful points.

QUESTIONS

The liberal use of questions encourages the client to work things out for himself. It is generally accepted that people retain information better when they have been actively involved in the process of gathering it. All the questions used in disputing are intended to help the client realise these 3 points:
1. Negative beliefs are not evidentially supported. They are not provable and hence are not facts.
2. Negative beliefs impede problem solving. Faulty thinking impairs functioning.
3. Negative beliefs produce unpleasant disproportionate emotional responses to negative events.

The following example questions can be used to both challenge negative beliefs and to support newer positive beliefs.

- What evidence do you have to support this belief?
- What proof can you give to support this belief?
- How does thinking this way lead you to behave?
- Is there any additional information you might be overlooking?
- Can you think of an alternative explanation for what happened?
- How is holding this belief helping you to reach your goals?
- If someone you really cared about held this belief what would you say to them?
- Would you recommend this way of thinking to a friend? If not, why not?
- How does thinking in this way leave you feeling?
- What would be a more constructive way of thinking about the situation?
- What effect does this way of thinking have on your overall mood?
- Although you strongly *feel* this belief to be true, can you entertain the possibility that you may be wrong?

ROLE-PLAY

Role-play is an effective means of reinforcing belief change. The therapist pretends to hold the client's negative beliefs and the client gets the opportunity to play therapist. By using arguments to convince the therapist to doubt her pretend negative beliefs and generate better alternatives, the client is effectively challenging his own beliefs. This is a core CBT skill that therapists strive to impart to clients. It is important to pitch the balance right between making it too easy or too difficult for the client to sway your thinking. Taking a step back from his own beliefs via role-play can help the client understand just how unproductive and ridiculous some of his thinking is.

Role-play can also be used to help clients rehearse acting in a new way. Unassertive clients often benefit from role-playing confrontational situations with their therapist in preparation for a real event.

OLD MEANING–NEW MEANING

CORE SCHEMATA are notoriously intractable, therefore it is good practice to employ more than one strategy to shift them. Since negative CORE BELIEFS are usually developed in early life they are typically formed as a result of certain types of unfavourable experiences. The meanings we attach to these early events are the essence of the beliefs we ultimately adopt. If meanings given to early experiences are not updated then negative beliefs formed at the time continue to inform our understanding of others, the world and ourselves.

This technique is intended to help the client revisit formative experiences and reassess assigned meanings from an older, more mature and better informed perspective. This exercise may need to be repeated several times in order to truly uproot ancient CORE BELIEFS. It is often used in session to give the client the added support of the therapist's guidance and input. It can be used as a homework assignment but it is imperative that the therapist allots sufficient time to reviewing and 'tweaking' the client's work. CORE SCHEMATA are customarily challenged in mid-stage treatment once the alliance has been established and more superficial COGNITIONS have been confronted. In some cases however, CORE BELIEFS are articulated fully in early sessions and can be tackled (with skill and professional sensitivity) straight away.

> **Illustrative example**: Megan's mother was a troubled woman and was not equipped to provide a secure environment for her daughter. Megan was frequently left unsupervised while her mother went out drinking with her friends. She recalls feeling constantly anxious that her mother would disappear one day and never come back. Megan stayed in the care of her mother until she was found wandering the streets unsupervised at age seven. She was then put into the custody of her maternal grandparents. Both grandparents seemed to resent Megan's presence and appeared to hold her responsible for her mother's abandonment. Unsurprisingly, Megan never felt that she belonged anywhere. Her grandparents' rejection and mother's abandonment led

Megan to conclude that she 'wasn't worth looking after'. Megan's CORE BELIEF about herself is that she is fundamentally worthless.

Below is a worked through 'old–new meaning' form based on the example of Megan.

EVENT	OLD MEANING	NEW MEANING
What happened? When? Who was involved?	What did it mean to you (or about you) at the time?	What is a more accurate meaning you can assign the event *now*?
1. Age 5, my Mum left me in the flat alone. She came back drunk (hours later) and told me off for crying.	1. I'm not important. I don't deserve to be looked after. Nobody cares about me.	1. Mum was an irresponsible parent. I deserved parental care like any child.
2. Age 9 or 10, my grandmother was angry. She told me that if it weren't for me, she and Grandad would be able to go on a cruise.	2. I'm in the way. I'm unwanted and worthless.	2. Gran and Grandad resented Mum leaving me in their care. Unfortunately they often vented their resentment on me.
3. Age 10, Grandad punished me for not washing up. He spanked me and said I was a 'bad child' who drove Mum to drink.	3. Everything is my fault.	3. I wasn't a 'bad child', I was a neglected child. Mum drank for her own reasons—it was not my responsibility.

Fig. 6.3 Old–New Meaning Form

Ascribing new meanings to old events is a powerful therapeutic experience for many clients. Very few people however, will notice an immediate positive effect on their emotions. It's as though there is a time lag between COGNITIVE RESTRUCTURING and improved mood. Although they are mediated by COGNITION, emotions take a while to 'catch up' with altered thinking. It takes time (and effort) for intellectual insight to impact on emotions. Dryden and Branch (2008) refer to this treatment stage, when the client *knows* a healthy belief is true but does not yet *feel* that it is true, as the 'head–gut' issue.

Emotions are a visceral experience. Unhealthy negative emotions seem to leave behind an affective residue. Hence behavioural reinforcement is essential for improved thinking to translate to improved mood. CBT therapists will ideally take care to explain this phenomenon to their clients.

ACTING 'AS IF'

When a client understands a new belief to be true and helpful but does not yet *feel* it to be true in their *gut*, the 'as-if' exercise is very useful. It works on the principle that acting in line with a belief serves to reinforce that way of thinking. It is difficult and uncomfortable for people to act in a way that contradicts a strongly held belief. The psychological term for this is COGNITIVE DISSONANCE. In order to reduce the discomfort experienced by COGNITIVE DISSONANCE, people will either make their behaviour consistent with their beliefs or modify their beliefs so that they are consistent with their actions.

For example, Frank believes that he is unlikable and that if he attempts to engage with others socially he is likely to be rejected. Frank is encouraged by his therapist to go into a social situation acting *as if* he truly believed that he were a likeable person. Frank goes to the local pub and makes eye contact with people, sits amongst others, makes small talk and maintains open non-defensive body posture. Through manifesting the *behaviours* of someone who thinks of him or herself as likeable, Frank begins to experience COGNITIVE DISSONANCE. The inconsistency between

Frank's negative self-opinion and his socially confident behaviour will force him to re-evaluate his belief. Frank also gets a chance to gather information that disproves his prediction that he will be rejected if he makes a social effort.

IMAGERY WORK

Imagery is used in several different ways in CBT treatment. Two of the many possible ways imagery can be used include:

- The client is asked to imagine holding a healthy belief with the aim of making the belief more 'real' to them. They are asked to imagine how their behaviour would be different if they were living with this new way of thinking. They may also be asked to imagine specific benefits arising from a changed belief.

- The client is asked to imagine a typical, vivid or recent example of a TRIGGER situation. The therapist encourages the client to imagine being in that same situation but with their new improved way of thinking. The idea is that the client will experience some degree of emotional change and/or be able to imagine using coping strategies effectively.

Negative mental images are often a maintaining feature of several of the ANXIETY disorders. CBT therapists may get the client to change the outcome of catastrophic images. For example, helping the client to visualise a more positive outcome whereby they cope with a difficult situation effectively.

People suffering from OBSESSIVE-COMPULSIVE DISORDER (OCD) frequently experience distressing intrusive mental images (Veale & Willson, 2004). The mental images (though unwelcome) are not themselves the problem. Rather the degree of emotional disturbance the client experiences in response to intrusive images is where the problem lies. OCD sufferers typically assign faulty meanings to intrusive thoughts and images such as 'normal people don't get these thoughts' or 'having these images pop into my head means that I'm bad and dangerous'. With this client population, CBT treatment involves helping the client accept the presence of unwanted mental activity and to reassign more benign meanings to unpleasant images.

CBT recognises the value in probing clients about images accompanying negative emotional states. Clients often neglect to report strong or recurrent images to the therapist. This may often be due to embarrassment, shame or simply not understanding that images are of clinical relevance.

The COGNITIVE techniques included in this chapter are by no means exhaustive. For more information refer to the recommended reading included in the appendix and texts listed in the references.

7

BEHAVIOURAL TECHNIQUES

Behavioural techniques feature largely in CBT treatment for virtually any type of psychological problem. Although considerable emphasis is placed on the maladaptive effects of faulty COGNITION in CBT theory, in actual practice it is often more expedient to begin treatment with behavioural interventions. In cases of severe depression for example, COGNITIVE change is often best achieved through behavioural modification in the first instance (Beck et al, 1979). As we touched on in Chapter 6, the reinforcing effects of certain behavioural compensatory strategies on negative beliefs and AVERSIVE EMOTIONS are not to be underestimated or ignored. Typically different types of emotional problems are associated with thematically consistent modes of thought and action. It therefore makes sense to consider these three areas—emotions, thoughts and behaviours—as part of an interactive system rather than as disparate entities. Targeting interventions at one of these areas is likely to encourage positive change in the other two and vice versa.

In this chapter we will look at the types of behaviour that maintain and perpetuate common emotional problems such as ANXIETY, depression and guilt. We also briefly describe the typical CBT interventions used to target problematic behaviours. Please bear in mind that this chapter is intended to provide a 'taster' or overview of behavioural interventions used in standard CBT treatment and is not a complete guide. We recommend further reading in the appendix, which discusses in detail the specialised CBT treatment protocols for specific disorders.

SAFETY BEHAVIOURS

SAFETY BEHAVIOUR is a term used to describe the lengths people will go to in order to keep themselves 'safe' from a predicted negative event. This term is particularly used in the assessment and treatment of ANXIETY disorders such as OBSESSIVE-COMPULSIVE DISORDER (OCD), phobias, social anxiety, agoraphobia and panic disorder. Because ANXIETY disorders are generally associated with an elevated expectation of imminent danger and a diminished perception of personal capacity to cope with a specific threat or danger, sufferers will develop (sometimes very elaborate) methods of avoiding 'risky' situations and reducing anxious feelings. Unfortunately these AVOIDANCE strategies (SAFETY BEHAVIOURS) serve to reinforce the idea that danger is around every corner and compound the sufferers' belief that they are unable to cope in ANXIETY-provoking situations. Rather than coming to realise that ANXIETY, though unpleasant, is survivable, the sufferer continues to believe that his SAFETY STRATEGIES are responsible for staving off a catastrophic outcome.

CBT practitioners will carefully investigate the SAFETY BEHAVIOURS an individual client is employing and help the client understand the detrimental effect they ultimately have on overcoming the target problem. In essence the client will be helped to realise that AVOIDANCE deprives them of the opportunity to experience different, more positive outcomes from what their ANXIETY predicts. Once this rationale is clear, the client is encouraged to enter situations that typically provoke his ANXIETY whilst dropping SAFETY BEHAVIOURS.

Below are some fictional examples of typical SAFETY STRATEGIES associated with OCD and panic disorder.

Illustrative example: Marsha has OCD about being contaminated by germs and making herself and her family sick inadvertently. She therefore washes her hands 20 to 30 times after doing tasks like emptying the bin or using the lavatory. Generally she avoids touching any food or kitchen utensils without wearing surgical gloves. Marsha also insists that her family change their clothes in the porch before entering the house. She then instantly washes the 'exposed' clothing and insists that the family shower straight away. Marsha will not allow visitors into the home for fear of contamination and avoids touching outsiders.

> **Illustrative example**: Harender suffers from panic attacks. These attacks have typically occurred in crowded places like on public transport and in shopping areas. Harender believes that she will be unable to breath and will collapse in public. She therefore avoids using any form of transport and walks miles to work. Harender also will not go into a shop by herself in case she collapses and needs help to get home. When she cannot avoid going out on her own, she uses nasal sprays to help her breath and stays near benches and rails in order to avoid collapsing.

MOOD-BASED BEHAVIOUR

According to the *DSM-IV-TR* (APA, 2004) classification system, mood disorders are a group of diagnoses where emotional disturbance is supposed to be the primary underlying feature. Mood-based behaviour refers to the tendency for an individual to act in accordance with a prevailing mood state. Behaviours borne out of depressed mood states such as social withdrawal, reduced activity and AVOIDANCE increase feelings of helplessness and hopelessness.

> **Illustrative example**: Cameron has been depressed for several months. She feels ashamed about her difficulty in executing everyday tasks that she used to find easy and even enjoyable. Cameron also puts herself down for needing professional help because she believes that her depression is all her own fault and that she should be able to pull herself together. She feels so helpless and hopeless that she spends most of her days in bed, avoiding phone calls, post and work. Cameron has lost contact with her friends and family over the months. She avoids any social outing and makes excuses to her family for not seeing them.

Cameron's example shows how mood disorders such as depression are worsened and perpetuated by mood-based behaviour. Unwittingly, Cameron is doing exactly what her depressed mood dictates thereby feeding her depression. Scheduling small manageable tasks into a depressed client's day is often a first step in the treatment of depression. Before trying to help the client get better, the CBT therapist first needs to stop the client from making herself worse. This is not to imply that the client is to blame for their low mood. It is very difficult to act against overwhelming negative feelings.

STRATEGIES TO AVOID NEGATIVE AFFECT

When a client holds rigid rules and beliefs he is vulnerable to intense uncomfortable feelings when those rules are broken. Therefore the client may develop behavioural strategies to avoid activating AVERSIVE EMOTIONS. Unfortunately such strategies reinforce unhelpful ways of thinking.

Illustrative example: Hal believes that if he 'lets down' his friends in any way then he is a terrible person for doing so. He never says 'no' to requests from friends because if he did, he would feel intense guilt. As a result, Hal often fails to act in his own best interests and frequently ends up doing things he doesn't want to do (or have time to do) for the benefit of others.

Because Hal understandably wishes to avoid discomfort associated with feelings of intense guilt he lets himself be pushed around. Instead of learning to bear his discomfort and challenge his belief that he must not let others down, his overly compliant behaviour reinforces this unhealthy attitude. In CBT treatment Hal would be encouraged to desist from behaviour designed to stave off aversive guilt feelings and modify his beliefs that produce disproportionate guilt in the first place.

This is just one example of an emotional state that individuals will make self-defeating efforts to avoid. Others may include shame, anger, ANXIETY, hurt and so on.

GOAL SETTING AND HOMEWORK

From the very first session, CBT treatment involves identifying specific emotional and practical problems that the client is grappling with. A problem list is developed and from this list, specific goals for therapy are developed. Goals in CBT are carefully negotiated between therapist and client to ensure that they are specific, measurable, achievable, realistic and time bound. These points for goal setting are represented by the acronym 'SMART'.

S: Specific. Goals pertain to specific examples of target problems. It is not sufficient for example, to accept a goal of 'feeling less anxious'. Where and when the client wishes to feel less ANXIETY needs to be precisely defined, i.e. 'to be able to go shopping in my local grocery store without feeling anxious'.

M: Measurable. There needs to be a mechanism for monitoring progress toward the specific goal. Sometimes psychometric measures can be used for this purpose; Beck's Depression Inventory (BDI) is commonly used to monitor severity of depression. SUBJECTIVE Units of Distress Scales (SUDS) can be useful when monitoring goal progression in ANXIETY disorders. Additional measures may include encouraging the client to keep a log of their progress. In this log the client can record even small positive changes that may otherwise be overlooked or quickly forgotten.

A: Achievable. Goals need to be within the client's scope to achieve. Essentially goals need to be tailored to meet the client's existing skills set. Any skill deficits need to be addressed and rectified where appropriate. For example, a client may need some assertiveness training. Additionally goals need to be dependent on the effort of the client himself. Goals that include changing other people's behaviour are not useful since others are not within the client's sphere of control. So a goal stated thus 'to stop other people from making unreasonable demands on me' is not acceptable whereas the goal 'to be able to assert myself in the face of unreasonable demands from others' is considered achievable.

R: *Realistic*. There is little point in accepting a therapeutic goal that realistically the client is unlikely to be able to achieve. To do so only sets the client up to fail. It is important to take into account the place the client is *starting* from when agreeing goals. Hence, if a client's extreme social ANXIETY leads him to avoid talking in social groups, it is not realistic to agree a goal of becoming a stand-up comic. A more realistic goal would be 'to be able to talk freely in small social groups'.

T: *Time bound*. Some goals will be short-term and others medium or long-term. It is not always possible to accurately estimate how long it will take an individual to realise their specific goals. It is prudent however, to place goals within some sort of time frame. Doing so lends structure to the treatment and promotes consistent client effort. CBT therapists need to exercise caution when setting time frames. Too long a period may discourage the client or lead to complacency. Too short a time frame may overwhelm the client or lead them to further feelings of hopelessness if they fail to meet the 'deadline'. Ideally time frames for goal achievement will be kept quite flexible so as to strike a balance between keeping the client motivated and guarding against possible self-recrimination.

The principle of INTERACTIONALISM and mutual reinforcement (as discussed in this chapter's introduction and in previous chapters) dictates that goals ideally ought to include both an emotional and functional component.

Using the fictional examples of Hal, Harender and Cameron outlined above, typical problems and goals may be composed thus:

Problem: Hal is unassertive and experiences severe guilt if he 'lets friends down'

Goal: For Hal to be able to say 'no' to friends' requests without feeling intense guilt

Problem: Cameron is depressed and has markedly reduced functioning

Goal: To keep to an activity schedule and alleviate feelings of depression

Problem: Harender suffers panic attacks in public places

Goal: To be able to go on public transport and into shopping areas whilst feeling nervous but not panicky

Problem: Marsha has OCD and will not touch food or kitchen utensils without wearing surgical gloves

Goal: To be able to make the family dinner without wearing gloves and to feel concerned but not unduly anxious about contaminating them with germs

Note that the hypothetical problems and goals listed above include both an affective and behavioural component. Goals stated with this dual emphasis afford the opportunity to work simultaneously on COGNITIVE RESTRUCTURING and behavioural modification. Not only is the client encouraged to re-jig their thinking *against* a pre-existing negative belief and in *support* of a healthier alternative, as in Harender's case 'I can't cope with ANXIETY-provoking situations' versus 'I can cope in ANXIETY-provoking situations despite uncomfortable feelings' but they are also encouraged to *experience* the truth of new beliefs through action. To continue with Harender's example, she practises holding her new coping belief *whilst* going on the underground thereby learning that although the journey was not pleasant she did, in fact, survive it without calamity. Harender's belief in her ability to cope with unpleasant feelings and difficult situations is enhanced and her notion that danger is imminent erodes. Through the repetition of such 'exposure' based exercises, belief change is deepened and anchored. This process is often referred to in CBT literature and basic psychological parlance as HABITUATION.

In light of the above, homework assignments will be collaboratively devised and agreed upon between therapist and client. Additionally the homework will follow logically from the session work and will promote goal attainment. As with goal setting, homework needs to be devised carefully. Dryden and Branch (2008) discuss the principle of setting 'challenging but not overwhelming' between-session assignments. To clarify, homework will ideally be sufficiently challenging to propel the client outside of his comfort zone but also be within range of what he is currently able to execute. It is common for CBT therapists to build a *graded hierarchy* with their clients. This involves identifying goal-related tasks and ranking them in order of perceived difficulty. The idea is to move up the hierarchy from the lowest to the highest-ranking items. The speed at which the client moves up the hierarchy will depend on several factors such as:

- Client willingness to experience short-term discomfort in order to achieve long-term gain
- Severity and duration of the client's presenting problem
- The quality of the therapeutic relationship
- The therapist ensuring that the client adequately understands the rationale behind behavioural work
- Other emotional/psychological problems that may become evident through behavioural work and require therapeutic attention (for example, shame is a common emotional obstacle to therapeutic progress)
- Environmental factors

The skilled CBT therapist will bear these factors in mind throughout treatment and be sensitive to their potential interference. Another important point to bear in mind with regard to behavioural interventions is that the client will be expected to carry out tasks which will, almost inevitably, cause him a degree of emotional discomfort. Whilst the ultimate goal may be to eliminate ANXIETY, guilt or depression, the road to this goal will be paved with effort and regrettably—pain. So, although it would be highly desirable that Cameron goes through the allotted tasks on her activity schedule without any discomfort, this is highly unlikely to be the case. Instead she will be urged to grit her teeth and pull herself from one task to the next despite her profound feelings of lethargy and hopelessness. Eventually it will become easier but it can take some time. Also Harender will be asked to agree to go into ANXIETY-provoking situations *whilst* feeling anxious and learning to *bear* those intensely uncomfortable feelings. Again, eventually Harender's belief in her ability to cope with anxious feelings will increase and her fear of certain circumstances will begin to diminish. Likewise, Hal will be encouraged to decline requests from friends but to also expect to feel very uncomfortable about it for sometime—until he gets used to saying 'no'. It takes time for COGNITIVE and behavioural change to result in emotional change. Emotion is rather like the last coach on the train.

The setting and reviewing of homework will frequently constitute the bulk of the middle phase of CBT treatment. The therapeutic benefits of between-session homework are manifold:

- Therapeutic learning is transported outside of the consulting room and into the client's daily life

- Therapy time is maximised through the use of between-session practice

- Client independence and ownership of the therapy is promoted

- The client adopts valuable coping strategies

- Therapy moves from the philosophical and cerebral toward the practical

- Much is to be learnt by both client and therapist through homework assignments be they 'successful' or 'unsuccessful'. (If the client fails to complete homework or execute it as outlined, then obstacles can be identified and dealt with accordingly)

- Thoughtful homework construction/review between therapist and client may indicate to the client that his therapist is truly interested in his recovery and thereby strengthen the alliance

The work CBT therapists expect their clients to carry out is neither easy nor painless. Thus the CBT practitioner needs to be empathic, and compassionately 'cajole' the client along. The client's successes and efforts ought never to go unnoticed by the CBT therapist. To this end, many CBT therapists encourage their clients to keep a positive data record in which they write down their efforts and the therapeutic rewards of their hard work. CBT trainees are sometimes invited to consider what they would be prepared to do in order to overcome their own difficulties. Would you ask a client to do something that you, as a therapist, would not be prepared to do yourself?

8

METHODS OF DISCOVERING
ASSUMPTIONS, RULES AND CORE BELIEFS

Examining assumptions, rules and CORE BELIEFS will normally take place after the client has really become familiar with the CBT model and is beginning to apply it to specific everyday problems. Ideally the client will have completed homework assignments aimed at spotting and challenging his NEGATIVE AUTOMATIC THOUGHTS (NATS) with some degree of success. Catching and arresting NATS serves to shake the foundations of underlying belief systems and may potentially render CORE BELIEFS more accessible to the client. Having done homework on NATS also helps to ensure that the client has sufficient confidence in the model and in his skills at applying it prior to unearthing more fundamentally held beliefs. If this is not the case, and deeper belief work begins hastily, the client may feel overwhelmed or endangered and react defensively. It is incumbent upon the CBT therapist to be sensitive to the client's state of readiness before commencing this and *all* stages of CBT treatment.

The therapeutic importance of being prudent about timing is made clear by Neenan and Dryden (2004: 161): 'To tackle these beliefs before this stage has been reached may result in clients feeling overwhelmed, threatened, distressed or resistant and lead to premature termination of therapy.'

ASSESSING ASSUMPTIONS AND RULES

Once the CBT therapist has satisfied herself that the client is ready to start working on assumptions and rules, one or more of the following strategies can be used.

If–then statements
Dysfunctional assumptions are frequently expressed in causal 'if *x* occurs then *y* follows' type language. Assumptions can also be articulated as conditional statements such as 'unless I accomplish *x* then *y* will surely follow'. The initial 'if' or 'unless' component of the assertion dictates what the client believes he must either

achieve or avoid. The secondary 'then' component outlines the negative event that the client believes will ensue should he fail to do so. For example:

> Unless I always please my husband, then he will leave me for someone else.
>
> If I hand in a report late, then my boss will fire me.
>
> Unless I am always cheerful and fun, then my friends will stop liking me.
>
> If I let others know I'm depressed, then they will lose all respect for me.

Perhaps the most commonly used method of eliciting faulty assumptions via an 'if/unless–then' statement is to provide the client with the 'if' component and allow him to fill in the blanks.

Illustrative example: Joe is a hard worker who does well at his job. He enjoys his work and socialises a lot with his co-workers. However, Joe doesn't have any work friends in whom he confides. Even when he is stressed out at work he makes a superlative effort to hide it from colleagues. Rather than ask for help or explain his difficulties to his manager, Joe will work late and come in early to get things done on time.

Therapist: *OK Joe, so you'd like to be able to ask for help when you need it at work. It sounds like that would help you to control your stress levels more effectively. Have you recently avoided asking for help at work?*

Joe: *Last week I had a project due that I really needed someone to give me a hand with. But I just couldn't bring myself to ask anyone.*

Therapist: *I see. Would you like to try and work out why it is that you couldn't bring yourself to ask anyone for help when you were struggling to get the project done?*

Joe: *Yes.*

Therapist: *OK. I'm going to provide you with the first half of a sentence and I'd like you to complete it for me. If I ask for help completing the project ...*

Joe: *... then my co-workers will know that I'm struggling. They'll see that I can't do everything on my own.*

Therapist: *And if they see your struggle and realise that you can't do everything on your own ...*

Joe: *... then they may think I'm not up to the job, I'd feel incompetent.*

Therapist: *What do you think about the endings you gave to those sentences I started? Any clues there about why you might be finding it so difficult to ask for help from others at work?*

Joe: *I think that unless I can do everything on my own without any help then it means that I'm incompetent.*

At this point the CBT therapist will advisably record the last statement Joe made and begin helping him to test out whether or not this assumption is wholly true and helpful.

It is worth mentioning that Joe's judgement of himself as 'incompetent' in the work domain may indicate an all-pervasive CORE BELIEF of incompetence. At this stage this is merely a hunch however. The CBT therapist may make a mental note of this for later investigation if deemed appropriate.

RECOGNISING THEMES

Another way of teasing out personal rules and assumptions is to look for recurrent themes in the client's automatic thoughts. Client and therapist review together daily thought records (DTRs) and ABC forms (see Chapter 6), which the client completed in several different situations. Frequently we find that the client is expressing the same sentiment in various different forms. Here are some examples of Joe's automatic thoughts that he recorded in his DTR.

Situation: Being given directions by a stranger
Thought: I should've been able to work that out myself

Situation: Elderly mother sick in hospital
Thought: I will look after her when she gets home rather than inconveniencing my siblings

Situation: Setting up a DVD player
Thought: I shouldn't need to refer to the instruction manual

Situation: Hosting a dinner party
Thought: I've got to make sure that everyone has a nice time

Joe's therapist spotted a theme in his automatic thinking, namely that Joe takes responsibility for doing things by himself without any external assistance. She then put this to Joe, thereby inviting him to extract the underlying rule for living embodied in his NEGATIVE AUTOMATIC THOUGHTS:

> Therapist: *Looking at this DTR, you seem to habitually expect yourself to be able to sort things out. Do you agree with that Joe?*
> Joe: *I suppose so. I guess I do normally try to do whatever needs doing by myself.*
> Therapist: *And if you aren't able to do whatever needs doing by yourself ...?*
> Joe: *I give myself a hard time; I think it means that I'm not up to much.*
> Therapist: *What exactly do you mean by 'not up to much'?*
> Joe: *That there's something wrong with me. I'm incompetent.*

After this brief exchange it becomes clear that Joe's MALADAPTIVE ASSUMPTION is 'if I can't do everything by myself then I am incompetent'.

HIGHLIGHTING IMPERATIVE STATEMENTS

Rules and assumptions often include imperatives such as 'should', 'must', 'ought to', 'need to', 'have to' and 'got to'. These imperatives are rigid and non-negotiable leaving no room for deviation or error. We can see some of these clearly represented in Joe's automatic thoughts in the preceding section. When a client starts articulating imperative statements about himself and his behaviour it is a generally reliable signpost to a strongly held rule for living. Almost invariably, there will be a perceived negative consequence or punishment attached to breaking a 'should/must' based personal rule. Often this will be an affective consequence such as guilt, shame or depression. The client may sometimes be more readily able to identify a negative self-evaluative consequence such as 'I'm incompetent' than an affective one. It is a circular argument however, since a negative self-appraisal leads to a negative emotional response and vice versa.

Urging clients to notice their 'should' statements is another way of helping them to identify unhealthy assumptions. In the following example transcript, Joe first gives an emotional consequence for breaking his rules. The therapist uses this information to ask further questions that reveal Joe's negative self-evaluation.

> Therapist: *Joe, I notice that you say that you* should *or* need *to be able to do things like find your own way when you're lost, look after your mother, give a fun dinner party and so on. Do you agree that you use a lot of firm 'no other option' type language with yourself?*
>
> Joe: *Since you mention it, yeah I do.*
>
> Therapist: *And what do you imagine would be the result if you failed to do what you believe you* should *or* need *to do? Perhaps focus on the example of looking after your mother after she gets out of hospital.*
>
> Joe: *I'd feel ashamed if I didn't look after her myself.*
>
> Therapist: *And what would be shame-provoking about not looking after her yourself?*
>
> Joe: *I have to look after her myself because I'm the one who should be there for her.*
>
> Therapist: *So if I can clarify, to your way of thinking, you* must *look after your mother yourself or ...*
>
> Joe: *I'm a useless son who is just letting her down.*

After this exchange Joe's assumption becomes clear. It is also becoming more evident that Joe readily resorts to labelling himself 'incompetent' or 'useless' both in the work and family domain. This lends greater credence to the hunch that this may be a CORE BELIEF.

CHARTING HIGHS AND LOWS IN MOOD

Because dysfunctional assumptions or rules are typically unyielding and extreme they tend to produce extreme (often disproportionate) emotional responses in clients when *either* met or unmet. It is often very useful to pay attention not only to the client's low mood but also to investigate what lay behind a 'high' mood. When a client is able to fulfil an assumption or live up to a personal rule, they may experience profound relief and even temporary euphoria. Simply because the client is feeling good doesn't mean that it is not for problematic reasons. Using the type of questioning represented in the fictional transcript below can be a very efficient method of getting to the bottom of a client's underlying belief system. We will return to the example of Joe for the sake of consistency and clarity.

Therapist: *So the dinner party went well Joe?*

Joe: *Fantastic, everyone was raving about what a great time they had the next day at work. The food turned out just how I wanted it to and everyone ate loads.*

Therapist: *Great. So how do you feel about the dinner turning out so well?*

Joe: *Amazing. I'm totally over the moon. I haven't felt so good in weeks. It's a real ego boost y'know?*

Therapist: *Well I'm glad that you're feeling so good at the moment. But can I ask you another question at the risk of putting a bit of a dampener on things? I'll explain my reasons in a moment.*

Joe: *Well, sure I guess. Go ahead.*

Therapist: *Thank you. How do you imagine you'd be feeling Joe, if the dinner hadn't been such a conspicuous success?*

Joe: *What do you mean? Like if it had been a real flop ...?*

Therapist: *Well, either a flop or even if it had just been sort of mediocre.*

Joe: *Uh ...*

Therapist: *Think about it for a minute; try to imagine it going less well. How do you think you'd be feeling right now?*

Joe: *I'd be gutted. I'd feel terrible about going into work and facing everybody. I'd want to apologise to all the guests for making such a mess of it.*

Therapist: *That sounds like a pretty extreme response for throwing a mediocre dinner party. What do you think?*

Joe: *I'd certainly feel extremely embarrassed and depressed about it, yeah.*

Therapist: *Well happily it was more than mediocre by all accounts. But the point I'm trying to make is that because you so strongly* believe *that you* have *to throw an excellent dinner party, you'd feel profoundly* distressed *if you failed to do so.*

Joe: *That's true.*

Therapist: *And because you* met *your rule about throwing an excellent dinner party you feel profoundly* good *about having done so.*

Joe: *That's true too. So are you saying it's not right for me to feel as good as I do?*

Therapist: *Not exactly. I'm trying to highlight to you the assumption that I think you hold, namely, 'if I throw an excellent dinner party then I'm an OK person'. Do you agree that you hold that type of assumption?*

Joe: *I do. So what does that mean about my good mood?*

Therapist: *Only that, as your therapist, I'd like to encourage you to feel great about the dinner party* itself *going well but to also understand that you would still be an OK person* even *if had been mediocre or indeed, flopped. Do you understand?*

Joe: *I think I'm beginning to.*

From this point the therapist would continue to discuss with Joe how currently his self-worth is contingent upon his underlying assumptions/rules being adequately met. Joe would then be encouraged to consider how modifying his rules would enable him to be more flexible and to adapt to negative events like throwing a duff dinner party *whilst* still being able to basically think well of himself as a person. Joe may be urged to chart his moods and search for the assumptions underlying extreme variations.

EXPOSING CORE BELIEFS

CORE BELIEFS can be conceptualised as being a layer beneath assumptions and rules, which are basically on the same level and used interchangeably. After NATS and assumptions have been elicited and restructured, CORE BELIEFS are the next target area. In contrast to assumptions, CORE BELIEFS tend to be stated as definitive facts. As discussed in Chapter 3, they pertain to idiosyncratic beliefs the client holds *to be unquestionably true* about himself, other people and the world. As such they are notoriously difficult therapeutic territory to navigate. Examples of three typical CORE BELIEFS follow:

Self: I am weak

Others: People are ruthless

World/life: Life is stacked against me

Not every client will desire to or benefit from working at the CORE BELIEF level. Some clients will be content to leave therapy after they have managed to change a few dysfunctional assumptions and experience associated symptom relief. In order to work effectively at the CORE BELIEF level, treatment will need to be long-term (perhaps a year or more in some cases) and client consent is essential. Under no circumstances should the therapist insist that the client remain in treatment post-improvement if the client does not wish to do so. Firstly, duration of treatment is essentially up to the client and secondly any form of coercion flies in the face of the principle of collaboration that underpins CBT practice.

That said, if a client wishes to work at a deeper level of COGNITION then there are various methods of pinpointing CORE BELIEFS available to the CBT therapist.

THE DOWNWARD ARROW

This method is also used to identify assumptions and rules. It involves eliciting AFFECT-LADEN thoughts, temporarily assuming that these thoughts are true and then further eliciting the meaning assigned to these thoughts until a baseline belief is revealed. The baseline belief arrived at following this process is likely to be core. Unlike when working at the level of NEGATIVE AUTOMATIC THOUGHTS, during the downward arrow technique thoughts are neither challenged nor answered back to, if they were it would arrest the downward progression of the arrow. The therapist asks brief meaning-focused questions designed to move the client further into the core of his thinking. Even if the therapist has hunches about the client's CORE BELIEFS based on earlier NAT and assumption work, she will keep these to herself during the downward arrow exercise. It is important that the client is afforded ample time to focus on the questions asked and that his answers are generated entirely from his own introspection.

In order to use this method effectively it helps to adhere to the following points:

1. Identify a specific situation or typical example of the target problem.
2. If the client has specified a negative emotional state then use this to drive your questioning in the first instance.
3. Use leading questions such as 'what then?' and 'if that were true then what would that mean?' to elicit further conclusions from the client.
4. When you seem to have arrived at an endgame, complete your questioning with 'and what would that mean about you?' or 'and what do you conclude about yourself in that case?' The client's response to this question will very likely be a CORE BELIEF about himself or herself.

The sample transcript below shows how Joe's therapist used the downward arrow technique to find his CORE BELIEF about himself that was triggering his ANXIETY about organising a forthcoming conference for his company.

Therapist: *So Joe, what specifically do you find* ANXIETY-*provoking about organising the conference?*
Joe: *Well, it's a really big event, really high profile.*
Therapist: *And what is* ANXIETY-*provoking about it being a high profile event?*
Joe: *That I might screw it up.*
Therapist: *And if you did screw it up, what would that mean?*
Joe: *That everyone would know I'd jumped in over my head.*
Therapist: *And if others knew you were in over your head it would mean ...?*
Joe: *That they think I'm useless, not up to the job.*
Therapist: *And if they did think that you were useless, what would you conclude about yourself?*
Joe: *That I'm crap, totally incompetent.*

In this case the downward arrow revealed a CORE BELIEF Joe holds about himself: 'I'm crap/incompetent'. The same technique can be used to discover CORE BELIEFS about others and the world.

REVIEW OF RELEVANT HISTORICAL EXPERIENCES

The CORE BELIEFS we hold today usually have tendrils reaching into the past. CORE BELIEFS are generally formed in early life as a result of a myriad of factors including: family learning, traumas, particularly salient experiences, societal influences, cultural and religious norms and influences from peers or other significant adults. Sometimes we fail to update our early belief systems. Our ideas about ourselves, others and the world remain frozen despite adult experiences and learning which may contradict their validity.

CBT therapists will often ask clients when they think a particular assumption or CORE BELIEF first occurred to them. Often the client will be able to recite an incident or series of incidents that led them to form specific conclusions about themselves and the world around them. This can be therapeutically invaluable, as the client is then able to revisit these early experiences and assign more accurate and helpful meanings to them, thus updating his dysfunctional CORE BELIEFS and assumptions (see Chapter 6).

When the client and therapist are still on a quest to unearth CORE BELIEFS, questions about the past can be equally useful. When Joe's therapist asked him about childhood and early life events that may have contributed toward his assumption that he must do everything on his own or view himself as incompetent, this is what she found out:

> *From the age of nine Joe went to a very well-regarded school where the emphasis was on academic excellence and personal development. Joe was often told that he 'must do better' (even when his grades were very much above average) but was never offered any additional support. He also learned that second place didn't really count for much. Joe remembers working as hard as he could to impress his teachers but never being able to reach the level of achievement they seemed to expect.*

> *Joe's father also attended the same school as a boy and did very well. He always encouraged Joe to be self-sufficient, leaving him to work out homework unassisted and to do chores about the house unaided even when it was evident that Joe was struggling. Joe frequently remembers perceiving his father's refusal to help him chop wood or write a book report as punishment for not being able to do it on his own in the first place.*

> *On one occasion Joe was having problems with his friends and confessed his unhappiness to his mother. He desperately wanted her reassurance and advice about how to deal with the fractures in his social group. He recalls his mother saying, 'Oh dear, I'm afraid you'll have to deal with it yourself Joseph, no one else can sort it out for you'.*

From these hypothetical early experiences it is fairly easy to see how Joe developed the belief that he must do things under his own steam and that should he fail to do so then he is intrinsically incompetent. Despite the fact that Joe's parents were probably acting in accordance with what they believed was best for Joe in the long run, he developed some very hindering ideas about himself.

This fabricated example illustrates that any type of early experience can ultimately lead to the formation of both adaptive and maladaptive beliefs. Care received from parental figures need not be deliberately abusive or malicious nor blatantly nurturing or benevolent to contribute to CORE BELIEF formation. Similarly, whilst extreme or unusual events do tend to significantly inform an individual's understanding of the world, mundane events repeated over time can also carry profound influential weight.

DELVING INTO MEANING

The idiosyncratic meanings clients give to their experiences can be effectively exposed through the downward arrow technique. Another very simple method of pinpointing CORE BELIEFS involves getting the client to fill in the blanks:

I am _____

Other people are _____

The world is _____

Sometimes CORE BELIEFS are fully articulated in the form of NEGATIVE AUTOMATIC THOUGHTS. Reviewing NATS may bring to light probable CORE BELIEFS such as 'Oh, I'm so useless', 'nobody likes me', 'people are out to get me' and so on. If these types of NATS are consistently recorded it can be useful to investigate how deeply the client believes them in order to determine if they are core.

These shortcuts can sometimes work very well. It is advisable however to use them either in conjunction with one of the other methods discussed above, or as a last resort when other methods have been unsuccessful.

IN CONCLUSION

The meanings assigned to events from the past theoretically result in CORE BELIEFS as we have seen in the example of Joseph above. Current, anticipated and recent events then reactivate these CORE BELIEFS. In essence, TRIGGER EVENTS activate NEGATIVE AUTOMATIC THOUGHTS and assumptions, which confirm and reinforce the apparent validity of negative CORE BELIEFS. Therefore COGNITION (beliefs, rules, assumptions) critically influence, and potentially *skew*, interpretation of events. This brief summary aims to re-emphasise the interactive relationship between event interpretation, COGNITION, emotion and behaviour.

9

RELAPSE PREVENTION AND ENDINGS

In this chapter we will discuss CBT's somewhat unique position on maintaining and safeguarding therapeutic gains through collaborative planning and troubleshooting. We will also look at how endings are structured and negotiated in CBT.

PLANNING FOR AND PREVENTING RELAPSE

Relapse prevention is an important part of the final phase of CBT treatment. In the spirit of helping the client to become his own therapist, during the middle and final stages of treatment therapeutic gains are revisited and consolidated. Psychological improvement is attributed to the client's hard work and perseverance. This is not only an accurate representation of how improvement has been achieved but it also bolsters the client's confidence in his ability to maintain his psychological well-being after regular CBT sessions have ended.

Generally CBT therapists will discuss openly with their clients the possibility of symptom resurgence or *relapse*. Whilst there is no harm (and certainly there may be benefit) in taking an optimistic stance toward the client's continued improvement, clinical experience suggests that some degree of relapse is likely in most cases. It is therefore important to prepare clients for possible setbacks en route to wholesome recovery. This preparation normalises relapse and helps the client to view setbacks as a common part of recovery rather than a return to square one. By endorsing this viewpoint the client can effectively predispose himself to feel disappointed but not utterly devastated in the event of relapse. The return of symptoms is distressing enough without the added fear that all that has been gained through treatment is now lost. Through thoughtful collaborative planning for the possibility of relapse, the client is more likely to view setbacks as an opportunity for valuable review and practice. Setbacks can also provide opportunities for further learning.

The term 'relapse prevention' is something of a misnomer. The name suggests that this stage of CBT therapy is aimed at simply preventing problems from returning. From what has been discussed above it becomes clear that there is more to relapse prevention planning than the term suggests. The aim is to not only *prevent* but also to prepare the client to *manage* and *overcome* relapse should it occur.

For clients with enduring or chronic problems such as OBSESSIVE-COMPULSIVE DISORDER (OCD), addiction, chronic pain or treatment-resistant depression, relapse prevention is paramount. In these cases relapse is unfortunately more likely to be the norm than the exception. Clients with chronic conditions are often helped to view managing their symptoms as a lifelong endeavour. Lifestyle changes, behavioural exercises and managing intrusive thoughts are some of the more important aspects of recovery for this client group. Continued regular practice is frequently found to be essential and is a predictor of sustained improvement. Maintaining positive change and being alert to early warning signs of problems returning is a key aspect of relapse prevention planning for every client but is of particular relevance to clients with chronic conditions.

The main points pertaining to relapse prevention (to be considered *alongside* the client) are divided into categories and outlined below. (There are also several ready-made relapse prevention forms in existence that the CBT therapist may choose to use.)

REVIEWING PROBLEMS AND GOALS

When striving to consolidate therapeutic learning and change, it pays to revisit the original problem/s and associated goal/s. This reminds both client and therapist of how much progress has been made since treatment first began. Review of this nature also highlights what the client needs to pay attention to when planning to prevent and surmount relapse. We strongly recommend being very precise when responding to the relapse prevention-related questions posed in this section and the sections following.

Throughout CBT treatment it is expected that the therapist will be highly specific. Specificity clarifies and solidifies points in an individual's mind; the client is more likely to retain concise specific points than vague concepts.

The following questions can be useful for client and therapist to answer together:

1. *What were the original presenting problems that brought the client to treatment?* These can be separated into emotional, behavioural, interpersonal and environmental or practical problem categories. Psychiatric diagnosis can also be noted if applicable.

2. *What goals were set in relation to these problems?* Goals can also be clearly outlined by separating them into the same categories: emotional, behavioural, interpersonal and environmental or practical.

3. *What goal-directed change has been made thus far?* Specificity is key.

4. *What are the benefits of therapeutic change/progress made thus far?* The payoffs of hard work and effort can be surprisingly easily forgotten and taken for granted. Reviewing the benefits of goal-directed activity can help to renew client motivation. Here again it is good practice to be highly specific about the areas where benefits have been experienced.

REVIEWING BELIEF CHANGE

Although not every client will have worked on modifying maladaptive CORE BELIEFS, most will have achieved some COGNITIVE RESTRUCTURING on the assumption level by the time therapy is terminated. Certainly most clients will have identified their thinking errors and NEGATIVE AUTOMATIC THOUGHTS. Even clients who have experienced primarily behavioural interventions (as in the case of panic disorder for example) and less overt COGNITIVE RESTRUCTURING will have altered critical attitudes. Most CBT therapists will have one eye on attitude and belief change when considering relapse prevention. Recapping on and reinforcing positive belief and attitudinal change is therefore a crucial aspect of relapse prevention planning. The following is a guideline for charting belief change.

What negative CORE BELIEFS have been identified (if applicable)?
- *Self:*
- *Others:*
- *World:*

What healthy alternative CORE BELIEFS have been established and strengthened through treatment (if applicable)?
- *Self:*
- *Others:*
- *World:*

What MALADAPTIVE ASSUMPTIONS and rules have been identified?

What ADAPTIVE ALTERNATIVE ASSUMPTIONS have been developed?

What thinking errors does the client typically make?

What realistic interpretations has the client devised to counteract his thinking errors?

What skills has the client acquired for 'answering back to' or challenging his NEGATIVE AUTOMATIC THOUGHTS (NATS)?

RECOGNISING TRIGGERS

TRIGGERS are events or circumstances that activate negative CORE BELIEFS and attitudes. As such, TRIGGER EVENTS tend to give rise to psychological distress or disturbance. The same TRIGGERS that sparked off a client's original problems are worth revisiting when constructing a relapse prevention plan. Through the course of treatment clients may develop 'immunity' to particular TRIGGERS that once caused them difficulty. Yet it is still worth acknowledging past TRIGGERS as potential problem areas in the future. It is also worth 'upping the ante' by encouraging the client to imagine different or more extreme scenarios that may be likely to trigger off unhealthy beliefs, emotions and behaviours. This gives the client the chance to fortify his therapeutic defences against relapse should such events actually occur. The following is a guideline for reviewing past TRIGGERS and highlighting potential ones.

What types of situations or conditions have typically triggered unhealthy CORE BELIEFS/MALADAPTIVE ASSUMPTIONS/NEGATIVE AUTOMATIC THOUGHTS or thinking errors?

- Past environmental TRIGGERS (i.e. illness, financial worry, work hassles, seasonal changes, household bills, moving house etc.)
- Past interpersonal TRIGGERS (i.e. relationship conflicts with family, friends, workmates etc.)
- Other past TRIGGERS

What are some possible TRIGGERS to look out for in the future?

- Possible environmental TRIGGERS
- Possible interpersonal TRIGGERS
- Other possible TRIGGERS

What destructive behaviours and coping strategies has the client used in the past?

What are more constructive coping strategies that have been developed through the course of therapy?

In addition to identifying specific TRIGGERS it is also important to compile a list of early warning signs that relapse is looming. For some clients relapse is a very gradual process and there is no singular event per se that stands out as a TRIGGER. Often collections of factors are responsible for symptoms returning. Nipping relapse in the bud involves recognising subtle changes in mood, behaviour and thinking before they become more extreme and problematic. Below are some questions that can be used to this end.

What early warnings signs may signal problems returning?
- Consider these areas: unhealthy negative emotions, mood variation, negative changes in thinking and behaviour.

What lifestyle changes may indicate the risk of relapse?
- Consider: work/life imbalance, withdrawal from social interaction, reduced communication/intimacy with significant others.

What physical signs may alert the client to possible relapse?
- Consider: sleep disturbance, increased/reduced appetite, lethargy, and illness.

Once early warning signs have been explored, the next step is to refresh the client's memory about what has been most useful in treatment. Usually whatever strategies helped the client to recover in the first place will work again in the event of a relapse.

What areas does the client need to keep working on in order to maintain his therapeutic gains?

Which specific CBT strategies aided the client most in overcoming his emotional/behavioural problems?

What helpful beliefs and attitudes does the client need to continue practising and strengthening?

What behavioural techniques has the client used to overcome his problems?

Where can the client go for additional support if he starts to struggle?
- Consider: mental health professionals, GP, family members, friends and support groups.

Some clients may decide to resume regular CBT sessions if they are unable to emerge from a period of relapse independently. Alternatively they may book a few 'top-up' sessions as a preventative measure. It is common practice for CBT therapists to include resumption of therapy in relapse prevention planning. Medication is also a consideration when dealing with relapse. If medication has helped in the past it is prudent to encourage clients to keep an open mind about using it again in the future if needed.

ENDINGS

Treatment duration is discussed and negotiated from the beginning sessions and throughout CBT treatment. The regular review of goals and therapeutic progress keeps treatment on track and implies that it is time-limited rather than open-ended. Depending on the clinical setting, there may be a set amount of sessions available. In this case the therapist may regularly remind the client of how many sessions remain in order to make the best use of therapeutic time. Of course relapse prevention planning in itself also addresses treatment conclusion. For these reasons therapy termination is very much 'on the table' from the outset, steadily preparing the client for an end to regular sessions.

CBT's collaborative emphasis means that client and therapist work together as a team to help the former overcome his difficulties. As such the client is an active participant in his own recovery and through the acquisition of skills and techniques effectively becomes his own therapist. Between-session practice via homework assignments increases client autonomy and self-efficacy. Indeed the overall structure and implementation of CBT diminishes client dependency. Therefore endings do not come as a shock or a surprise to most CBT clients but are experienced as part of a natural progression. Generally termination does not result in a particularly emotive response on the part of either client or therapist. In fact, many CBT clients seem to prefer a businesslike end to their treatment. Certainly CBT therapists exhibit appropriate warmth toward their clients when saying goodbye and many will express how rewarding it has been working with them if this is the case. Clients of CBT also will frequently offer thanks for the help they have received but most clients will also recognise their own part in the process. In many cases therapy endings are not unlike endings with any other service-providing professional.

That said, certain clients might find the prospect of leaving treatment more daunting than others. Common client concerns include worry that they won't be able to cope as well once treatment has ended and fears that they still have outstanding issues, which may bring about relapse. In these instances the CBT therapist will take special care with relapse prevention planning. Additionally the therapist will strive to bolster client confidence and work gently but steadily on reducing client dependency on the therapeutic relationship. As we mentioned in the above section, CBT therapists will generally be flexible (where possible) about when to end treatment based on the client's circumstances and progress.

CBT clients are frequently offered 'top-up' sessions if deemed appropriate as part of their termination/relapse prevention plan. The client is urged to feel free to come back for a single session or series of sessions should they find themselves struggling anytime post-treatment. As normal treatment progresses, and the client becomes increasingly self-sufficient, sessions are tapered down to fortnightly, monthly or even longer intervals. This again prepares the client for a gradual arrival at permanent therapy termination and simultaneously leaves the door open for a commonplace resumption of sessions if and whenever necessary.

10

COGNITIVE BEHAVIOUR THERAPY
TRANSCRIPT

CBT therapy is active-directive and therefore the therapist will be involved in asking direct questions with a view to building a conceptualisation of the client's difficulties from the first session. Whilst the client will of course be given space to ventilate and outline their difficulties, the CBT therapist will be listening with a keen ear and will help the client to see their problems more clearly within an ABC FRAMEWORK. This may be done overtly or more discreetly within the first session. The CBT therapist will endeavour to socialise the client to the CBT treatment protocol as early as appropriate by encouraging them to make a problem list and formulate associated goals to target during therapy sessions. In the first session the CBT therapist will use core counselling skills such as active listening and reflecting to help build an alliance but he will also seek specific information and may even pose hypotheses about the client's emotional problems without delay. Every initial session will vary in content and structure to some extent, based on: the amount of information the therapist has received about the prospective client from the referral source; the severity of the client's problem; the level of training and experience of the CBT therapist; and the particular personality and communication style of both therapist and client.

Below is a mock transcript of a first CBT session. It is based on what actually takes place in real clinical sessions but is not a verbatim transcript. Rather we have collated aspects of several client–therapist interactions to produce a fictional example of a typical initial/assessment session of CBT. Sections of the transcript will be numbered and the corresponding interventions the therapist is making at these points will be explained.

The following is an account of Jason's first session with a CBT therapist. He has been referred by his GP for work-related stress and is meeting with his therapist (female) in a NHS surgery setting. 'T' stands for therapist and 'C' for client, in this case Cecile and Jason respectively.

T: Hello Jason, nice to meet you, I'm Cecile, a CBT therapist here at the surgery.

C: Hi, nice to meet you.

T: Your GP has sent me a referral for you stating that you're experiencing stress at work, is that correct?

C: Yes it is. I'm a junior accountant in quite a well-respected firm in the city. I've been having trouble coping lately.

T: Right, I see. OK, before we get stuck into the session are there any questions you'd like to ask me about CBT generally or the way I work?

C: Uh, not that I can think of … not really, no.

T: All right. If anything comes up during the session then please feel free to interrupt me and ask anything that may be on your mind. OK?

C: Sure. Thanks.

T: Have you ever had any therapy or counselling before Jason?

C: I saw a counsellor at uni for a few sessions because I was getting really depressed and strung out about exams. But that was about five years ago now. Nothing since.

T: And did you find seeing a counsellor helpful at that time?

C: Yeah, it was good to have someone OBJECTIVE to talk to.

T: Sure. Anything you can remember about your sessions that was particularly useful when it came to sitting your exams?

C: Uh, he gave me some practical techniques to use to improve my revising, making a study schedule and taking regular breaks. I found that really did help actually.

T: Sounds like good advice. So, do you think you'd like a problem-solving approach to therapy then?

C: Yeah, I guess so.

1T: Well that's great because CBT is a very focused and active type of therapy. I'll work with you to really nail down your specific problems and come up with goals related to them. Together we'll develop therapeutic tasks for you to do between sessions to assist you in reaching your goals. How does that sound to you?

C: That sounds good. I've really had enough of this depression and worry now. I really need to do something about it.

T: So roughly how long have you been feeling depressed and worried Jason?

C: About two years it's been really bad, you know, interfering with my work ... but I guess it's been there most of my adult life, like at uni as I mentioned. I've been in this job for three years or so and I was never really totally comfortable but yeah, past 18 months or so it's really reached a peak. Sometimes I just can't go in to work, I call off sick. That's not good is it? I mean I don't want to lose my job.

2T: No, I can understand that. Can you tell me more about when you typically get anxious at work? Maybe give me a recent or typical example of a situation that you found ANXIETY-provoking?

C: We have a team meeting every week on Wednesdays and everyone is expected to give a brief rundown of what's happening in their area, updates and proposed solutions to any problems—you know?

T: Yep, carry on ... and you feel anxious in those meetings?

C: Totally anxious, I can't stand everyone focusing on me when it's my turn to speak. Sometimes I'll say as little as possible or even go into work late so I miss the team meeting. I just hate it.

3T: So you do your utmost to avoid speaking in team meetings because of your intense anxious feelings. What *exactly* is it about speaking up in meetings, all eyes on you, that you get most anxious about?

C: I'll say something stupid or not be able to answer a question, make a general tit of myself.

4T: And if you did fail to answer a question or say something stupid, what thoughts do you have about that?

C: Everyone will lose respect for me and think I'm incompetent.

5T: What would it mean about you if your colleagues

considered you incompetent?

C: They'd be correct.

6T: You'd silently agree with them is that right?

C: Yeah, which is crazy because I know I'm pretty good at what I do. I mean I get decent results, I'm reliable, apart from lately when I've been too panic-stricken to go in, but I still meet deadlines and all that.

T: You're confident that you do a good solid job but in those moments when you're anxious about saying something stupid in front of your co-workers you lose sight of that and focus on their potential judgement of you as incompetent, is that how it works Jason?

C: Yes, and I think of myself as an incompetent tit.

T: Which can't be very pleasant either I'm guessing ...

C: (Laughs) No. In fact it's pretty ...

T: Depressing?

C: Yeah.

7T: OK Jason, let me feed this back to you to see if I've got it straight. I'll put it in a CBT format called an ABC and explain as I go, OK? You jump in and put me right if I've got anything we've just discussed wrong, OK? It's important that I get this in your own words and that it makes sense to you.

C: Fire away.

8T: OK, I'm going to write this down so we can both have a look at it together. The situation, that's A in the ABC is team meetings where you generally have to speak in front of other co-workers and managers, right?

C: Yep.

9T: Your thoughts about that situation, B in the ABC FRAMEWORK, are that you may say something stupid or be unable to provide an answer to a question and thus your colleagues will lose respect for you because they will see you as incompetent. Is that right so far?

C: Sure is.

10T: Now C in the framework stands for consequences like behaviours, feelings and further thoughts. In your example you feel intense ANXIETY, that's your feeling or emotion. You also avoid speaking in front of others at work by calling in sick, coming in late and so on, that's your behavioural consequence. Correct?

C: Indeed.

T: And your quiet belief that if others think of you as incompetent then it *proves* that you *are*, that goes at B as well. Let me just write that in …

C: And that's what I get depressed about, if I make a gaff I think about what a tit I am and how stupid and ridiculous I am for having this fear of talking aloud, how I always make a tit of myself.

11T: So you put yourself down Jason, not only for any gaffs you may make, but also for being fearful or anxious in the first place? Thus depressing yourself?

C: That's right. Because it *is* pathetic and stupid to be so bloody anxious about such a little thing that everyone else can do without even thinking about it. Isn't it?

12T: Well, I'm going to have to disagree with you here Jason. Care to hear why?

C: Sure.

13T: Well, your ANXIETY is undoubtedly unpleasant and inconvenient but I don't agree that you're either stupid or ridiculous as you say, for having an ANXIETY problem. Rather I'd suggest that you're just a normal imperfect person—like everyone else on the planet. How does holding that damning view of yourself help you?

C: I used to think that it inspired me to pull myself together but talking about it now I realise that I just end up feeling depressed.

14T: I see, so what you're saying is that putting yourself down as 'an incompetent tit' only serves to lower your mood, is that right?

C: That's correct.

15T: Can you see how refusing to put yourself down about your ANXIETY will actually help you to focus on overcoming it?

C: I suppose so, because I'll feel less depressed and hopeless.

16T: That's what I think too. And looking at the ABC again (referring to whiteboard or paper) can you see how your thoughts at B are leading to your ANXIETY at C?

C: Uhm, my thoughts about being considered incompetent are making me anxious about speaking in the meetings.

17T: That's exactly right. So if you were to make a gaff and *not* assume automatically that everyone thinks of you as incompetent, what effect do you imagine that would have on your anxious feelings?

C: I imagine I still wouldn't like making a gaff and I may still feel a little nervous about talking, uh, but perhaps I wouldn't be as anxious as I am now. I would probably be more willing to attend team meetings if I really were able to imagine that other people aren't always on the verge of judging me as incompetent.

18T: I agree with that too. Now, at the moment isn't it true that you don't actually *know* for sure that your co-workers will judge you incompetent if you mess up but that you assume or *infer* that will be their judgement of you?

C: That is true … they could think lots of other things I suppose, like 'better you than me mate' or even feel a bit sorry for me, maybe even think that it's like, out of character for me to make a gaff based on what they know of my usual performance.

T: True. They could think a myriad of things in response to your gaff; do you think it's possible that some of them might not even think much about it at all? You know, just sort of be indifferent to it?

C: Possibly. Yeah, that may well be a possibility. They may have other more important things on their minds than my performance. Maybe they have their own lives to focus on … yeah.

T: Good point. And what about your own view of yourself as an incompetent tit? Do you have to draw that conclusion about yourself or could you choose to draw a more accurate one when you do make mistakes at work, or even *imagine* making a gaff at work for that matter?

C: I don't have to call myself a tit. But it's difficult to imagine
      not feeling like one anyway. I could try to take the view
      that to err is human, like you touched on earlier. I don't
      know that I believe that though to be honest.

19T: Believing it usually comes with time and practice. So
      trying to act according to the belief that 'mistakes are
      regrettable but don't render me an incompetent tit' is likely
      to reinforce the truth of that idea in your mind.

C: I guess so.

T: You sound hesitant. What's on your mind?

C: Well, you make it sound so easy but I honestly don't know
      where to begin.

20T: I'm glad you told me that and I'll try to clarify things for
      you. What happens when you avoid meetings? Does your
      ANXIETY disappear?

C: Only temporarily. Until the next Wednesday.

21T: And let me ask you Jason, what's your goal for this
      problem we've been talking over? How would you like to
      see things resolved?

C: I want to be able to talk in meetings and in front of the
      board, whatever, anything my job entails without totally
      losing the plot and running scared. I don't want to be
      depressed all the time about how this problem is stifling
      my career advancement.

T: OK, if I just attempt to précis that: your goal is to attend
      meetings, speak up and to do so with little or minimal
      ANXIETY, thus advancing your career. That right?

C: Exactly so.

22T: And how is AVOIDANCE helping you to reach that goal?

C: OK, you got me Cecile, it's not. Not at all.

23T: Why not?

C: Because I just keep going in a vicious circle and I never
      face up to my fears.

T: So based on this ABC and our talk so far, what do you think
      might help you to reach your goal? What might you need
      to think and do differently to realise your goal?

C: I need to get my ass into meetings and speak up despite how anxious I may be about the possibility of screwing up in some way.

24T: Yep. And what if you do screw up? What attitude or belief will help you cope with that possibility?

C: Everyone screws up from time to time? I'm not an incompetent tit just because I screwed up?

T: Very true. But what about your colleagues' and superiors' judgements of you?

C: Uh, probably not everyone is judging me as incompetent and a tit. Some may not be even that interested in me.

T: True again Jason. And let me just be the fly in the ointment here, what if some of them *do* think you're incompetent on the basis of a gaff in a meeting situation? What then? Are they right?

C: Actually no. They're wrong, one or even twenty mistakes is just human dammit. Isn't it? Isn't that what we've been driving at?

T: It is. And you're right. How much do you actually believe that making mistakes is forgivable, regrettable and human?

C: More than I did a few hours ago. It's beginning to sink in.

T: Excellent. How about we look at what tasks you can do between now and next session to strengthen that way of thinking and bring you closer to your goals?

C: OK. Let's do that.

INTERVENTIONS EXPLAINED

First let us just reiterate that this is a fictional truncated transcript and not representative of an entire therapeutic hour. Therefore it is important to bear in mind that CBT doesn't always progress as quickly and smoothly as represented here, although it can.

Secondly, during a genuine assessment session the therapist will gather more background information about the client than is represented in this transcript. We have omitted life history exploration because it is typical of any psychotherapeutic approach and is not a distinctive feature of CBT.

Thirdly, in a real assessment session the client may ask the therapist about her experience of dealing with his particular type of problem or may enquire about the therapist's level of training and qualifications. CBT practitioners will answer such questions openly and honestly.

1T: Cecile, the CBT therapist, is socialising Jason to the active-directive approach of CBT. She describes setting specific goals and introduces the concept of between-session homework. Finally she asks Jason for feedback.

2T: To get a better understanding of Jason's ANXIETY, the therapist asks for a recent or typical example.

3T: Here Cecile is summarising the behavioural consequences of Jason's ANXIETY. (AVOIDANCE is also termed a 'SAFETY BEHAVIOUR' in CBT.) She then begins to elicit the most ANXIETY-provoking feature of meetings to Jason's mind.

4T: Cecile is investigating NEGATIVE AUTOMATIC THOUGHTS, inferences and assumptions that Jason may have about saying something 'stupid'.

5T: This question aims to elicit the evaluative meaning Jason assigns to being poorly thought of by his colleagues.

6T: Cecile confirms that Jason considers or labels himself incompetent when he infers that his colleagues are judging him similarly.

7T: Cecile begins to summarise the information gathered thus far into an ABC FORMAT. She tells Jason that she is about to do this, thus preparing him to listen to her explanation of his ANXIETY. Cecile also takes care to invite input from Jason, which may help refine the conceptualisation.

8T–10T: The situation of speaking in meetings is placed at A. Jason's inferences that others will judge him incompetent and his negative self-evaluation are placed at B. Both emotional consequences and behavioural consequences (ANXIETY and AVOIDANCE) are recorded at C.

11T: Jason's comments indicate a secondary emotional problem of depression. Cecile feeds this back to Jason for clarification. This question is posed in such a way to underscore the CBT position that thoughts lead to emotions.

12T–15T: Here Jason's depression-creating beliefs about his primary ANXIETY are challenged. Jason shows understanding and thus therapy is refocused on the ABC. In reality, resolving a secondary emotional probl₋m that is obstructing progress on the primary problem would be likely to take much longer.

16T–18T: Cecile helps Jason to see that his beliefs at B about the situation at A lead to feelings of ANXIETY at C. They then investigate and challenge Jason's negative self-evaluations and inferences at B together.

19T: Jason is expressing understanding about how his ANXIETY problem is perpetuated and maintained but is unclear on what action to take next. Cecile validates his confusion and offers to help make things clearer. She uses SOCRATIC QUESTIONS to enable Jason to draw his own conclusions.

20T: Goals relating to Jason's ANXIETY are developed.

21T–22T: Cecile's questions are aimed at helping Jason to recognise behavioural and attitudinal changes that will help him overcome his ANXIETY.

23T–END: Time is spent on reinforcing the shifts in Jason's thinking and ample time is devoted to devising and planning suitable homework. Though not represented in this transcript, Jason would also be asked for feedback on the session and encouraged to ask questions or express any doubts or reservations.

11

APPLICATIONS OF

COGNITIVE BEHAVIOUR THERAPY

In the 1950s Albert Ellis became dissatisfied with the results he was getting using PSYCHOANALYSIS with his patients. Ellis turned his attention to developing his own therapeutic approach based on his clinical experience and extensive knowledge of human psychology. RATIONAL Emotive Therapy (RET) was thus born (Ellis, 1994). Ellis's views on treating human disturbance were quite radical at the time. PSYCHOANALYSIS dominated and recognition of RET was hard won. Ellis successfully used RET to treat clients with emotional disorders and sexual problems. In later years the name was changed to RATIONAL Emotive Behaviour Therapy (REBT) to accurately reflect the behavioural component of this approach.

Aaron T. Beck responded to Ellis' innovations in psychotherapy and in the 1970s founded COGNITIVE Therapy (Beck, 1976). Through the continued work of Beck, Ellis and others, CT evolved and developed to become COGNITIVE Behaviour Therapy, as we know it today. (Chapter 1 in this primer provides a more in-depth examination of CBT's historical antecedents.)

GROWING POPULARITY

There has been a real surge of interest in CBT over the past few years. Though widely used and accepted as efficacious for well over a decade, CBT now seems to be the buzzword on everyone's lips. Alex McMahon, head of the mental health delivery unit with the Scottish Government, announced a £3 million programme for CBT in Scotland, during the British Association for Behavioural and COGNITIVE Psychotherapies' (BABCP) annual conference held in Edinburgh this July.

In addition to growing popularity in the UK, CBT is also widely practised in America, Canada and throughout Europe. Part of CBT's success is certainly due to its extensive evidence base. Proven efficacy and relative brevity in comparison with other approaches make CBT an economical treatment strategy. The following article, taken from the BABCP website, sums up the UK government's current commitment to psychological therapies and CBT in particular.

> The BABCP today warmly welcomed Health Secretary Alan Johnson's announcement of a £170 million expansion in psychological therapies.
>
> BABCP President David Veale said the announcement would increase access to CBT for hundreds of thousands of people and mean more than 3,000 new therapists would be needed. Dr Veale said:
>
>> This is fantastic news for all those people who have been waiting for access to CBT. It will mean a massive expansion of CBT right across the country with thousands more therapists trained and employed.
>>
>> This is probably the single biggest step forward in the provision of CBT that we have ever seen in Britain. It also means that mental health is now taking centre-stage and being recognised by the Government as a major issue for our times.
>>
>> This announcement is a tribute to the BABCP, as the lead organisation for CBT in the UK and for a host of other mental health organisations who have been campaigning with us for an expansion of therapy for years. We are delighted.

The Government will next year (2009) roll out psychological therapies to twenty new areas before increasing services to cover the whole country over the next few years. Health Secretary Alan Johnson, who was speaking on World Mental Health Day, said:

> More than one in six people suffer from mental health problems at any one time. For many people prescribing medication is a successful treatment but we know that psychological therapies work equally well.

Today's announcement shows the government's commitment to mental health. Improving access to psychological therapies will give people with mental health problems a real choice of treatment, helping to reduce dependence on medication.

Psychological therapies, such as CBT, have proved to be as effective as drugs in tackling common mental health problems and are often more effective in the longer term. NICE guidelines on treatment for depression and ANXIETY recommend therapies such as CBT.

Building on the two demonstration projects at Newham and Doncaster, by 2010/11, the NHS will spend £170m per year on psychological therapies, with more than £30m in 2008/09 and more than £100m in 2009/10. Over the next three years, this investment in Improving Access to Psychological Therapies (IAPT) will mean:

- 900,000 more people treated for depression and ANXIETY
- 450,000 of them are likely to be completely cured (as expected with NICE guidelines)
- 25,000 fewer people with mental health problems on sick pay and benefits
- 3,600 more newly trained psychological therapists giving evidence-based treatment
- all GP practices having access to psychological therapies as the programme rolls out
- average waiting for psychological treatments down from the current 18 months to a few weeks (in line with urgent outpatient waiting times in the rest of the NHS) as the service rolls out

Lord Richard Layard, co-author of the London School of Economics Depression Report, who has campaigned for an expansion in CBT, said: 'This is great news and just what we've all been waiting for. Mental health is the biggest social problem in our country. This new service will bring relief from misery to millions of people.'

Psychiatric conditions

Increasingly CBT is being cited as the psychological intervention best used for treating a number of common psychiatric conditions. The National Institute for Health and Clinical Excellence (NICE) produces guidelines for optimum treatment outcome. CBT is specifically indicated in the NICE guidelines for treatment of the following disorders:

- Generalised ANXIETY disorder
- ANXIETY disorders including social phobia, panic, agoraphobia and other phobias
- Depression
- Post traumatic stress disorder
- Body dysmorphic disorder
- OBSESSIVE-COMPULSIVE DISORDER
- Anorexia, bulimia and atypical eating disorders
- Chronic fatigue syndrome
- Schizophrenia

This is of course good news for CBT practitioners. More training courses are opening up in universities all over the UK (see appendix for details) and research continues. CBT is being tailored to suit specific disorders like those listed above as a result of research findings. Though the basic theory remains unchanged, emphasis is placed on whichever interventions and techniques work best with specific client populations.

New wave CBT

New therapies based on CBT theory and principles have developed over recent years. Many of these are developing evidence bases of their own and popularity is growing. Special interest groups for several of these 'new' therapeutic methods have been formed as offshoots of the BABCP. It is not possible to go into great depth about these therapies in this chapter. However the more prominent ones are listed below:

- Mindfulness Based CBT (MBCBT): Based on CBT principles and mindfulness meditation, this approach has been found effective for treating depression. For more information about mindfulness you can read *Full Catastrophe Living* by Jon Kabat-Zinn.

- Schema-Focused Therapy (SFT): Developed by Dr. Jeffery Young; this approach focuses on the treatment of personality disorders.

- Acceptance and Commitment Therapy (ACT): Steven Haynes is the foremost expert on ACT. This approach has been used to treat chronic pain and emotional disorders. You can find out more on the Association for Contextual and Behavioural Sciences (ACBS) website.

- Behavioural Activation (BA): This approach has proved highly effective for the treatment of depression. To find out more read *Manage Your Mood* by David Veale and Rob Willson.

- Meta-Cognitive Therapy (MCT): This approach is becoming increasingly popular and is being researched extensively. MCT focuses on the appraisals made by individuals about their thoughts. For more information on MCT, consult work by Adrian Wells.

SETTINGS

CBT is practised in private and NHS hospitals both in group and one-to-one settings. Increasingly psychiatric nurses are being encouraged to take further training in CBT. GP surgeries sometimes offer individual CBT counselling and, as we can see from the above article, this is likely to increase under the government's new mental health initiative.

Counselling services within the voluntary sector are also moving toward CBT. Many charity-run alcohol and drug rehabilitation units are using CBT either in conjunction with or in favour of the traditional 12-step approach.

The use of CBT with children and young people is an area for potential growth. It is already used in America and the UK to treat children suffering from OBSESSIVE-COMPULSIVE DISORDER. It would be good to see CBT move into school counselling programmes in the future.

There are numerous CBT self-help books on the market. Individuals can use these books to find out more about CBT, help themselves overcome problems or use them in conjunction with professional CBT treatment. Computerised CBT is also becoming more readily available and it will be interesting to see how this develops in the next few years.

There are many private CBT practitioners in the UK. A list of accredited therapists is available from the BABCP website.

12

RESEARCH INTO
COGNITIVE BEHAVIOUR THERAPY

COGNITIVE Behaviour Therapy is probably the most researched psychotherapy model. In fact it is so well researched that it becomes difficult to decide what to include in a single chapter. This chapter will therefore be kept brief and instead of citing a plethora of studies we will advise on where to access research papers.

PROVEN EFFICACY

CBT is perhaps best known for its effectiveness in the treatment of depression and ANXIETY disorders. This has been borne out in many studies including: Rush et al, 1977; Blackburn et al, 1981; Murphy et al, 1984; Salkovskis and Warwick, 1986; Teasdale et al. 1984, to cite but a handful.

The Royal College of Psychiatrists recently noted that CBT has been found:
- most effective for conditions where ANXIETY and depression is the main problem
- most effective for moderate to severe depression
- as effective as antidepressants for most types of depression

As has already been mentioned in the previous chapter, the National Institute for Health and Clinical Excellence (NICE) recommends CBT as the preferred psychological intervention in treatment guidelines for a host of psychiatric disorders. In order for NICE to authorise a specific treatment the approach needs to be proven effective through randomised controlled trials. This speaks to the thorough scientific rigor CBT research has managed to achieve. Research into the effectiveness of CBT for many different types of disorders is on-going. The incorporation of emerging research results into existing theory and practice keeps CBT a vibrant and contemporary therapy.

WHERE TO FIND OUT MORE

For up-to-date research papers the *Behavioural and Cognitive Psychotherapy* journal, Cambridge University Press, is an excellent source. This journal is distributed to all BABCP members. Other useful sources include:

Cambridge Journals Online <journals.cambridge.org/bcp>
Institute of Psychiatry <www.iop.kcl.ac.uk>

APPENDIX

RESOURCES FOR LEARNING

ORGANISATIONS

Albert Ellis Institute (AEI)
   <www.albertellisinstitute.org>
Association for Contextual Behavioural Science (ACBS)
   <www.contextualpsychology.org>
British Association for Cognitive and Behavioural Psychotherapies (BABCP)
   <www.babcp.com >
UK Council for Psychotherapy (UKCP)
   <www.psychotherapy.org>
National Institute for Health and Clinical Excellence (NICE)
   <www.nice.org.uk>
Institute of Psychiatry (IOP)
   <www.iop.kcl.ac.uk>
Royal College of Psychiatrists (RCP)
   <www.rcpsych.ac.uk>

CBT TRAINING

Goldsmiths, University of London
University of Derby
University of Sheffield
Institute of Psychiatry, King's College, London
Oxford Centre for Cognitive Therapy
The Albert Ellis Institute, New York, NY

FURTHER READING

Bennett-Levy, J, Butler, G, Fennell, M, Hackman, A, Mueller, M, & Westbrook, D (eds) (2004) *Oxford Guide to Behavioural Experiments in Cognitive Therapy*. Oxford: OUP

Burns, DD (2000) *The Feeling Good Handbook* (2nd rev ed). New York: Plume

Dryden, W (ed) (2007) *Dryden's Handbook of Individual Therapy* (5th ed). London: Sage.

The Overcoming Series. London: Constable & Robinson

Neenan, M & Dryden, W (2004) *Cognitive Therapy: 100 key points.* Hove and New York: Brunner Routledge

Wells, A (1997) *Cognitive Behaviour Therapy for Anxiety Disorders*. London: Wiley

Willson, R & Branch R (2005) *Cognitive Behavioural Therapy for Dummies*. London: Wiley

WEBSITES

Mood gym teaches CBT techniques for overcoming depression and anxiety

   <www.moodgym.anu.edu.au>

No Panic offers advise and support for all types of anxiety disorders

GLOSSARY

ABC FORMAT/FRAMEWORK/MODEL   A structured format used throughout CBT therapies where A represents a TRIGGER EVENT, B represents thoughts and beliefs and C represents emotional, COGNITIVE and behavioural responses.

ACTIVATING EVENT   An event, either external or internal—actual or perceived, which triggers underlying beliefs and results in an emotional response. Represented as 'A' in the ABC FORMAT (see above).

ADAPTIVE ALTERNATIVE ASSUMPTIONS   Immediate thoughts in response to ambiguous or negative events based on personal rules for living. ADAPTIVE ASSUMPTIONS are functional in that they lead to constructive behaviour. These are developed through therapy to replace pre-existing MALADAPTIVE ASSUMPTIONS that perpetuate emotional disturbance and destructive behaviour.

ADAPTIVE BEHAVIOUR   A constructive behaviour (or change in behaviour) enabling adjustment to circumstance.

ADAPTIVE COGNITION   See above. Thoughts which promote healthy emotional responses and adjustment to aversive events.

AFFECT LADEN   Emotionally charged aspects of an individual's thoughts or experiences.

ALLIANCE CONCEPTS   Ideas and principles related to the therapeutic relationship.

ANXIETY   An emotional response when faced with real or perceived threat, risk or danger.

ATTENTIONAL BIAS   The tendency to focus on one or more aspects of a given situation to the exclusion of all other aspects.

AVERSIVE EMOTIONS   Extreme or inappropriate emotional responses to events which impede problem solving and overall ability to function effectively.

AVOIDANCE   The desire or tendency to avoid thoughts, situations or events which are likely to give rise to uncomfortable emotions and/or physiological responses.

BEHAVIOURISM   A school of OBJECTIVE psychology and philosophy which rejects SUBJECTIVE EXPERIENCE and consciousness. It states that the only relevant, valid psychological events are those which can be observed, i.e. behaviour.

CASE CONCEPTUALISATION   The process of collecting information from the client and building a picture of their problems using elements of the ABC FRAMEWORK.

CLASSICAL CONDITIONING   A process of behaviour modification using an unconditioned stimulus and a conditioned stimulus to produce a conditioned response. Using Pavlov's experiment as an example, food (unconditioned stimulus) produces salivation (unconditioned response). After repetition of combining food with the sound of a bell, the bell becomes a conditioned stimulus eliciting salivation (conditioned response).

COGNITION   The mental action of acquiring knowledge through perception and experience. Any type of thought is a COGNITION.

COGNITIVE Refers to the process of thinking.

COGNITIVE DISSONANCE   The state of having inconsistent thoughts, beliefs, or attitudes, especially as relating to behavioural decisions and attitude change.

COGNITIVE RESTRUCTURING   The process of helping a client to change their thinking and belief systems in order to promote psychological health.

COGNITIVE VARIABLES   Mental activity that accounts for variations in psychological, emotional and behavioural responses.

COLLABORATIVE EMPIRICISM   The process of client and therapist working together to gather evidence for and against a specific client belief.

CONDITIONING   To train or accustom an animal or human being to respond in a prescribed manner when confronted with a specific stimulus. See also CLASSICAL CONDITIONING and OPERANT CONDITIONING.

CONGRUENCE   One of the CORE CONDITIONS postulated by Carl Rogers. In CBT, therapist verbal and non-verbal behaviours are consistent with the message they wish to impart to the client.

CORE BELIEFS   Deeply held beliefs that inform an individuals understanding of themselves, other people and the world around them.

CORE CONDITIONS   Elements of the therapeutic relationship deemed necessary and sufficient to promote therapeutic change as postulated by Carl Rogers. These form the basis of person-centred therapy.

CORE SCHEMATA   See CORE BELIEFS.

COUNTER-TRANSFERENCE   The emotional response of the counsellor to a client in psychodynamic therapy.

DIDACTIC TEACHING   The psycho-educational component of CBT. The therapist explicitly sets out to educate the client about core principles of CBT.

DISPUTATION   The process of using empirical, logical and pragmatic arguments to encourage the client to reassess the validity of their problematic beliefs.

EMPATHY   The ability to understand and share the feelings of another person. One of the CORE CONDITIONS postulated by Carl Rogers.

HABITUATION   The diminishing of a psychological or emotional response through frequent exposure to a stimulus.

INFERENTIAL   Refers to conclusions made on the basis of reasoning and gathering evidence. In CBT terms client inferences may be faulty due to the influence of MALADAPTIVE ASSUMPTIONS and CORE SCHEMATA.

INTERACTIONALISM   Refers to reciprocal action and influence between actual events, COGNITIVE processes and emotions.

IRRATIONAL BELIEFS   Personal demands that certain conditions must exist. IRRATIONAL BELIEFS are postulated by Albert Ellis to underpin all types of emotional and psychological disturbance.

LIKERT SCALE   A scale used in the sciences to measure spectrum-based phenomenon. Generally constructed from 0–10 where 0 represents the extreme low end of the spectrum and 10 represents the extreme high end.

MALADAPTIVE ASSUMPTIONS   See ADAPTIVE ALTERNATIVE ASSUMPTIONS.

MALADAPTIVE BEHAVIOUR   Counterproductive behaviour (or change in behaviour) that impedes adjustment to circumstance.

NEGATIVE AUTOMATIC THOUGHTS (NATS)   Negative and self-defeating thoughts that seem to spontaneously occur in response to an ACTIVATING EVENT.

OBJECTIVE   Impartially considering and representing the facts of an event without being influenced by personal feelings or beliefs.

OBSESSIVE-COMPULSIVE DISORDER (OCD)   A psychiatric condition characterised by obsessive intrusive thoughts and/or compulsive performance of ritualistic behaviour.

OPERANT CONDITIONING   A process of behaviour modification conditioned through positive or negative reinforcement, and largely determined by consequences.

PRIMARY PREVENTION RESEARCH   Looking at the factors which predispose people to certain conditions/distress, such as social and environmental conditions, and personal characteristics and experiences.

PSYCHOANALYSIS/PSYCHOANALYTIC   School of psychology originated by and based on the work of Sigmund Freud.

PSYCHOPATHOLOGY   The study or manifestation of mental (psychological) disorder (pathology). A term originating in the medicalisation of distress.

QUALITATIVE (concept)   An idea relating to a quality that cannot be measured precisely. For example, a red ball, a happy occasion, a frightening experience.

QUANTITATIVE (concept)   An idea relating to a quality that can be measured precisely. For example, six inches of rain, a temperature of ninety-two degrees.

RATIONAL BELIEFS   Personal preferences that certain conditions ideally exist. RATIONAL BELIEFS lead to healthy psychological adjustment and emotional responses if conditions are not met. See also IRRATIONAL BELIEFS.

RECONCEPTUALISATION   The process of reviewing an original CASE CONCEPTUALISATION and refining it in light of new information. See also CASE CONCEPTUALISATION.

SAFETY BEHAVIOURS/STRATEGIES   Behaviours and methods used by the client to prevent activating uncomfortable emotions and psychological responses.

SOCRATIC QUESTIONING   The process of using questions to encourage clients to think for themselves thereby guiding them toward a therapeutically relevant conclusion.

SUBJECTIVE EXPERIENCE   The understanding of a personal experience based on idiosyncratic beliefs, thoughts and emotions. (Dependant on personal perception.)

THERAPEUTIC ALLIANCE   The quality of the professional relationship between therapist and client. See also CORE CONDITIONS.

THINKING BIASES   The tendency to repeatedly think in ways consistent with an underlying belief about the self, others and the world. Also refers to faulty information processing.

THOUGHT–FEELING LINK/INTERACTION   Refers to the mutually reinforcing relationship between thoughts and emotions.

TRANSFERENCE   The process in which a client imputes thoughts and feelings in the analyst which actually refer to previous important figures (usually parents) in the client's life.

TRIGGERS   See ACTIVATING EVENTS.

UNCONDITIONAL POSITIVE REGARD   One of the CORE CONDITIONS postulated by Carl Rogers. The therapist maintains a non-judgemental and accepting attitude toward the client.

REFERENCES

American Psychiatric Association (2004) *Diagnostic and Statistical Manual of Mental Disorders-IV-TR* (4th edn, text revision). Washngton, DC: APA.

Bandura, A (1977a) *Social Learning Theory.* Englewood Cliffs, NJ: Prentice Hall.

Bandura, A (1977b) Self-efficacy toward a unifying theory of behavioural change. *Psychological Review, 84,* 191–215.

Beck, AT (1976) *Cognitive Therapy and the Emotional Disorders.* London: Penguin.

Beck, AT, Emery, G & Greenberg, RL (1985) *Anxiety Disorders and Phobias: A cognitive perspective.* New York: Basic Book.

Beck, AT, Rush, AJ, Shaw, BF & Emery, G (1979) *Cognitive Therapy of Depression.* New York: Guilford Press.

Beck, J (1995) *Cognitive Therapy: Basics and beyond.* New York: Guildford Press.

Bennett-Levy, J, Butler, G, Fennell, M, Hackman, A, Mueller, M & Westbrook, D (eds) (2004) *Oxford Guide to Behavioural Experiments in Cognitive Therapy.* Oxford: Oxford University Press.

Blackburn, IM, Bishop, S, Glen, AIM, Whalley, LJ & Christie, JE (1981) The efficacy of cognitive therapy in depression: A treatment trial using cognitive therapy and pharmacotherapy, each alone and in combination. *British Journal of Psychiatry, 139,* 181–9.

Blackburn, IM & Davidson, K (1990) *Cognitive Therapy for Depression and Anxiety.* Oxford: Blackwell Science.

Burns, DD (1990) *The Feeling Good Handbook.* New York: Plume/Penguin.

Clark, DA, Beck, AT & Alford, BA (1999) *Scientific Foundations of Cognitive Theory and Therapy of Depression.* New York: Wiley.

Clark, DM & Fairburn, CG (eds) (1997) *Science and Practice of Cognitive Behaviour Therapy.* London: Oxford University Press.

Davies, E & Burdett, J (2004) Preventing 'schizophrenia': Creating the conditions for saner societies. In J Read, LR Mosher & RP Bentall (eds) *Models of Madness: Psychological, social and biological approaches to schizophrenia.* London: Routledge, pp 271–82.

Dobson, KS & Block, L (1988) Historical and philosophical bases of the cognitive behavioral therapies. In KS Dobson (ed) *Handbook of Cognitive Behavioral Therapies.* New York: Guilford Press, pp 3–38.

Dryden, W & Branch, R (2008) *Fundamentals of Rational Emotive Behaviour Therapy,* London: Wiley.

Dryden, W & Rentoul, R (eds) (1991) *Adult Clinical Problems: A cognitive behavioural approach.* London, New York: Routledge.

Ellis, A (1994) *Reason and Emotion in Psychotherapy: A comprehensive method of treating human disturbances.* New York: Birch Lane Press.

Gilbert, P & Leahy, RL (eds) (2007) *The Therapeutic Relationship in Cognitive Behavioural Psychotherapies.* London: Routledge.

Hackman, A (1998) Cognitive therapy with panic and agoraphobia: Working with complex cases. In N Tarrier, A Wells & G Haddock (eds) *Treating Complex Cases: The Cognitive Behavioural Therapy approach.* Chichester: Wiley, pp 27–45.

Hawton, K, Salkovskis, P, Kirk, J & Clark, DM (eds) (1989) *Cognitive Behaviour Therapy for Psychiatric Problems: A practical guide.* Oxford: Oxford Medical Publications.

Meichenbaum, D (1969) The effect of instruction and reinforcement on thinking and language behaviours of schizophrenics. *Behaviour Research and Therapy 7,* 101–14.

Meichenbaum, D (1985) *Stress Inoculation Training.* New York: Pergamon Press.

Murphy, GE, Simons, AD, Wetzel, RD & Lustman, PJ (1984) Cognitive therapy and pharmacotherapy singly and together in the treatment of depression. *Archives of General Psychiatry, 41,* 33–41.

Neenan, M & Dryden, W (2004) *Cognitive Therapy: 100 key points.* Hove and New York: Brunner-Routledge.

Padesky, CA (1993) Schema as self-prejudice. *International Cognitive Therapy Newsletter,* 5/6, 16–17.

Padesky, CA & Greenberger, D (1995) *Clinicians Guide to Mind Over Mood.* New York: Guildford Press.

Padesky, CA & Mooney, KA (1990) Presenting the cognitive model to clients. *International Cognitive Therapy Newsletter, 6,* 13–14.

Pavlov, IP (1927) *Conditioned Reflexes.* London: Oxford University Press.

Persons, JB (1989) *Cognitive Therapy in Practice: A case formulation approach.* New York: WW Norton & Co.

Rachman, SJ & Wilson, GT (1980) *The Effects of Psychological Therapy* (2nd ed). Oxford: Pergamon.

Rogers, CR (1957) The necessary and sufficient conditions of therapeutic personality change. *Journal of Consulting Psychology, 21,* 91–103. Reprinted in H Kirschenbaum & VL Henderson (2000) *The Carl Rogers Reader.* London: Constable, pp 219–35.

Rush, AJ, Beck, AT, Kovacs, M & Hollon, S (1977) Comparative efficacy of cognitive therapy and imipramine in the treatment of depressed outpatients. *Cognitive Therapy and Research, 1,* 17–37.

Safran, JD & Segal, ZV (1990) *Interpersonal Process in Cognitive Therapy.* New York: Basic Books.

Salkovskis, PM & Warwick, HMC (1986) Morbid preoccupations, health anxiety and reassurance: A cognitive-behavioural approach to hypochondriasis. *Behaviour Research and Therapy, 24,* 597–602.

Teasdale, JD, Fennell, MJV, Hibbert, JA & Amies, PL (1984) Cognitive therapy for major depressive disorder in primary care. *British Journal of Psychiatry, 144,* 400–6.

Trower, P, Casey, A & Dryden, W (1988) *Cognitive Behavioural Counselling in Action.* London: Sage.

Veale, D & Willson, R (2004) *Overcoming Obsessive-Compulsive Disorder.* London: Constable and Robinson.

Watson, JB & Rayner, R (1920) Conditioned emotional reactions, *Journal of Experimental Psychology 3,* 1–14.

Wells, A (1997) *Cognitive Therapy of Anxiety Disorders: A practice manual and conceptual guide.* Chichester: John Wiley.

Wills, F & Sanders, D (1997) *Cognitive Therapy: Transforming the image.* London: Sage.

Young, JE, Klosko, JS & Weishaar, ME (2003) *Schema Therapy: A practitioner's guide.* New York: Guilford Press.

INDEX

PCCS Books

the independent publisher
for independent thinkers

www.pccs-books.co.uk

Website features include:

- Permanent discounts

- Free UK delivery

- Personal accounts

- An information resource

Support your specialist independent publisher

Tel: +44 (0)1989 763900
Fax: +44 (0)1989 763901
Email: contact@pccs-books.co.uk

The

Cognitive Behaviour
Counselling
Primer

**Rhena Branch
and
Windy Dryden**

PCCS BOOKS
Ross-on-Wye

First published in 2008

PCCS BOOKS Ltd
2 Cropper Row
Alton Road
Ross-on-Wye
Herefordshire
HR9 5LA
UK
Tel +44 (0)1989 763 900
www.pccs-books.co.uk

The Cognitive Behaviour Counselling Primer

A CIP catalogue record for this book is available from the
British Library

ISBN-13 978 1 898059 86 8

Cover design by Old Dog Graphics
Printed by Athenæum Press, Gateshead, UK